W9-AVH-124

$40°°

HINTS

ON

PUBLIC ARCHITECTURE

HINTS

ON

PUBLIC ARCHITECTURE,

CONTAINING, AMONG OTHER ILLUSTRATIONS,

VIEWS AND PLANS OF THE SMITHSONIAN INSTITUTION:

TOGETHER WITH AN

APPENDIX RELATIVE TO BUILDING MATERIALS.

PREPARED, ON BEHALF OF THE BUILDING COMMITTEE OF THE SMITHSONIAN INSTITUTION,

BY

ROBERT DALE OWEN,

CHAIRMAN OF THE COMMITTEE.

DA CAPO PRESS • NEW YORK • 1978

Library of Congress Cataloging in Publication Data

Owen, Robert Dale, 1801-1877.
    Hints on public architecture.

    (Da Capo Press series in architecture and decorative
art)
    Reprint of the 1849 ed. published by Putnam, New York,
issued as Publication P of Smithsonian Institution.
    1. Washington, D.C. Smithsonian Institution
Building. I. Title. II. Series: Smithsonian Institution. Publication; P.
Q11.093 1978   727′.6′09753   77-17509
ISBN 0-306-77545-X

This DaCapo Press edition of Robert Dale Owen's *Hints on Public
Architecture* is a replica, slightly reduced in page size, of the original
edition, published in 1849. This second edition is limited to one
thousand copies, of which five hundred, numbered 1 through 500,
are facsimile bound and privately distributed by the Smithsonian
Institution.

This is copy number ——————.

Introduction © 1978, by Cynthia R. Field

DaCapo Press, Inc.
A Subsidiary of Plenum Publishing Corporation
227 West 17th Street, New York, N.Y. 10011

All rights reserved

Manufactured in the United States of America

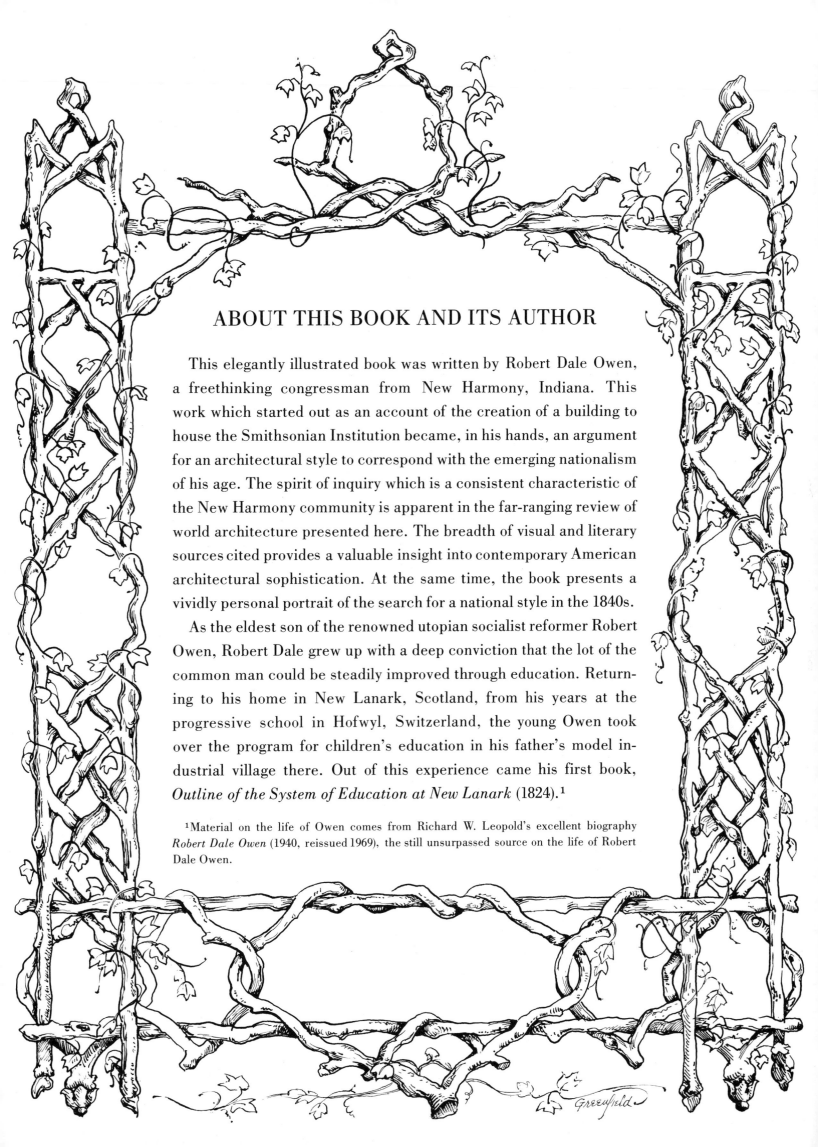

ABOUT THIS BOOK AND ITS AUTHOR

This elegantly illustrated book was written by Robert Dale Owen, a freethinking congressman from New Harmony, Indiana. This work which started out as an account of the creation of a building to house the Smithsonian Institution became, in his hands, an argument for an architectural style to correspond with the emerging nationalism of his age. The spirit of inquiry which is a consistent characteristic of the New Harmony community is apparent in the far-ranging review of world architecture presented here. The breadth of visual and literary sources cited provides a valuable insight into contemporary American architectural sophistication. At the same time, the book presents a vividly personal portrait of the search for a national style in the 1840s.

As the eldest son of the renowned utopian socialist reformer Robert Owen, Robert Dale grew up with a deep conviction that the lot of the common man could be steadily improved through education. Returning to his home in New Lanark, Scotland, from his years at the progressive school in Hofwyl, Switzerland, the young Owen took over the program for children's education in his father's model industrial village there. Out of this experience came his first book, *Outline of the System of Education at New Lanark* (1824).[1]

[1] Material on the life of Owen comes from Richard W. Leopold's excellent biography *Robert Dale Owen* (1940, reissued 1969), the still unsurpassed source on the life of Robert Dale Owen.

In 1825 father and son took up residence in the United States where Robert Owen, expanding upon his concept of a communal society, had established a utopian community at New Harmony in southwestern Indiana. This most ideal of societies failed to flourish, yet the town of New Harmony continued as a unique amalgam of intellectual and scientific activity.

Between 1827 and 1833 Robert Dale Owen became a leading proponent of liberal ideas both as a newspaper editor and public speaker in New Harmony and New York City. He opposed debtors' prisons and capital punishment, intemperate drinking, and slavery and advocated adult education, free schools, and free thought. His opposition to organized religion was well known. As spokesman for the rights of women and laborers, he was in the vanguard.

His particular concern for improving the economic status of women led Owen to publish a pamphlet entitled *Moral Physiology; or, a Brief and Plain Treatise on the Population Question* (1830) which was the first American birth control manual. Later that year he published a series of six essays on "Public Education," arguing that the instruction of all children be supported by the states through their power of taxation. In a remarkably short time he had become a controversial figure identified with both liberal and radical causes. For the next three years Owen devoted himself to family and community affairs in New Harmony. Two more literary efforts were published, *Discussion on the Existence of God and the Authenticity of the Bible between Oregen Bacheler and Robert Dale Owen* (1831) and *Pocahontas: A Historical Drama in Five Acts* (1837).

Elected to the Indiana State House in 1836, Owen continued to work for social reform but the single-minded fervor of his youth came to be tempered with the art of political compromise learned in three years of service to his state. In 1842 he went to Washington as the representative from the First District of Indiana. In his two terms as a congressman Robert Dale Owen participated actively in the important debates of his day concerning issues of national expansion, among them the Oregon boundary dispute and the annexation of Texas. His long standing interest in educational matters inspired him to become a leader in the campaign to establish the Smithsonian Institution.

When John Quincy Adams had finally pushed Smithsonian legislation through the Senate in February of 1845, the bill went to the House of Representatives where Owen immediately proposed an alternate measure and became the head of a Select Committee on the Smithsonian. A great deal of oratory had already been spent on the proper institution to realize the bequest of James Smithson for "the increase and diffusion of knowledge among men." Rufus Choate imagined a world-renowned library; John Quincy Adams, an astronomical observatory. Joseph Henry, soon to become the first secretary of the Institution, would later propose a scientific research center. Owen, for his part, envisioned a national free university making education available to all. Addressing the 29th Congress, he declared:

> We must reach the minds and hearts of the masses; we must diffuse knowledge among men; we must not deal it out to scholars and students alone . . . over the entire land must the rills from this sacred fountain freely flow; not to be arrested and walled up here, to minister to our pleasure or convenience. We greatly mistake if we imagine that our constituents are indifferent to the privilege of drawing from these waters of knowledge; that they cannot appreciate their fertilizing influence. If there be one feeling more powerful than another in the hearts of the millions in this land, even through its remotest forests, it is that the intellectual cultivation which circumstances may have denied them shall be secured to their children.[2]

Owen's visionary thinking leaped ahead of legislative debate to focus on the building which would both house and represent the Smithsonian Institution. In August of 1845 he wrote to his brother, geologist David Dale Owen, asking for a "well digested plan," expecting that David Dale would "consult utility first, in the various internal arrangements, and let architectural elegance follow as a secondary, though not unimportant, consideration."[3] He sent along a sketch of plans developed by Robert Mills in 1840 for a National Institute or a Smithsonian Institution, which showed the linear arrangement with stairtowers and the medieval English style subsequently used in the building. In October of 1845 David Dale Owen returned detailed plans for a building in the "Norman" style having a large central pavillion linked to side pavillions by "cloisters," furnishing "an agreeable promenade for students, professors, and visitors."[4] Two years later William Seaton of the Executive Committee made a point of stating

---

[2]*Documents Relative to the Smithsonian Institution,* William J. Rhees, editor, (1880), April 22, 1846, p. 347; also *Congressional Globe,* 20th Congress, 1 Session, Appendix 471.

[3]Robert Dale Owen to David Dale Owen, August 15, 1845, in Correspondence, Explanatory of the Details of a Plan of Buildings for a Smithsonian Institution Prepared by David Dale Owen, M.D., Workingmen's Institute, New Harmony, Indiana.

[4]*Ibid,* David Dale Owen to Robert Dale Owen, October 10, 1845.

that "general internal arrangements of that plan were substantially adopted . . . one of the present wings is a copy, somewhat modified, of the original elevation submitted by him (Dr. O), yet that he (Dr. O) received no remuneration. . ."[5]

When the act establishing the Smithsonian was finally passed, Robert Dale Owen made himself a central figure as a member of the Regents' Executive Committee, Planning Committee, and Building Committee. The Regents met for the first time on September 7, 1846, for a summary session. By September 9th, Owen, Seaton, and Joseph Totten, had been elected as the total membership of the Executive Committee for the Institution, and the Owen plan had been presented to the Board. At the same time a committee was organized which became the Building Committee, consisting of the Chancellor of the Board of Regents, the Secretary of the Institution (as yet unelected), and the members of the Executive Committee, who were authorized to obtain plans for the building, to purchase books, to visit sites, and to hire consultants.

Knowledge of the building plans was already abroad, as Washington builder William Archer, having apparently heard of the impending commission, took this opportunity to present his plan, drawings, and cost estimates for a proposed Smithsonian Institution building. On the 22nd day of September, 1846, the resolution creating a Building Committee was published in the newspapers of Washington as a means of notifying architects of the commission.

Eager to get ahead with the work, a subcommittee led by Owen took matters into their own hands, entering upon a personal tour of principal cities to see well-known buildings, confer with architects, and collect building materials and data for cost estimates. In Philadelphia, they visited the famous Girard College, the Eastern Penitentiary, the Mercantile Exchange, the Customs House (formerly the Bank of the United States), and other buildings. William Strickland and Thomas U. Walter were called upon, but were absent. John Haviland was also absent, but John Notman spent a good bit of time visiting with the committee and accompanying them to the city of Trenton, where they viewed the lunatic asylum and the renovated statehouse. In New York City, a number of churches were visited, including the Gothic Grace Church and the Romanesque Church of the Pilgrims by James Renwick, Jr. Renwick was

[5]*The Smithsonian Institution: Journals,* William J. Rhees, editor, (1879), "Reports of the Building Committee," August 27, 1847, p. 690.

consulted on more than one occasion, frequently in the company of his father, the well-known professor James Renwick, who was a friend of Joseph Henry. Other architects consulted were Richard Upjohn, Owen Warren, Martin Thompson, Joseph Wells, and David Arnot. Quarries in the New York area were visited to sample the building materials. In Boston the group visited the Athenaeum, the Customs House, the Merchants' Exchange and other structures. The architects consulted were Isaiah Rogers and Ammi B. Young. Cincinnati was also visited, apparently by Owen alone en route to New Harmony. While there, he visited with the architects Howard Daniels and Henry Walter. Thus, in a comparatively short period of time, Owen and his associates made themselves familiar with most of the major monuments of recent construction in the United States. Buildings of varied styles were visited, ranging from the pure Greek Revival of Girard College to the Gothic of the Eastern Penitentiary. All the architects with whom Owen and the Board conferred were invited to submit their plans to the Board by the 25th of December at the latest.

Well before the deadline, on the 30th of November, 1846, the Building Committee reported in their minutes that the plans of James Renwick, Jr., had been selected out of the thirteen plans submitted by architects for the building. They recommended to the Board the adoption of Renwick's design, done in the late Norman style, also referred to in the text as the Lombard style. The first mention of the book which would become *Hints on Public Architecture* occurred in the report at the same time with the statement that the Board of Regents had authorized publication by the Building Committee of a "small volume, which will give to the public the design of the building, and all important particulars regarding materials, etc."[6]

By December 1846 suspicion that the architect had already been chosen was widespread. Many of the well-known designers involved were actively dissatisfied with the course of the competition. Two pamphlets protesting Owen's handling of the procedure—one by William Elliot, and another by David Arnot[7]—were published, condemning what they regarded as favoritism in the

[6]*Ibid,* "Journal of Proceedings of the Board of Regents," November 30, 1846, p. 7.

[7] William Elliot, untitled printed letter, A.J. Davis Collection, Metropolitan Museum of Art, New York, Manuscript Division. David Henry Arnot, *Animadversions of the Proceedings of the Regents of the Smithsonian Institution in Their Choice of an Architect.* New York, 1847.

selection of James Renwick, Jr. And indeed there was some truth in these allegations. While undeniably his was the most sophisticated design among the surviving submissions, Renwick was particularly favored in being allowed to upgrade his presentation after seeing the other designs. Owen declared openly that Renwick's plan had been selected and was being revised to meet economic strictures even as other Regents declared no plan had been adopted.[8]

The matter of the architect was not, however, laid to rest. Some members of the Board, especially Seaton and Hilliard, pressed to have the architects heard before final action was taken by the Board. This being accomplished, the Board moved swiftly to reconsider the earlier resolution. Acrimonious debate followed for several days. Finally, on January 28th, 1847, Owen was able to effect the passage of a resolution naming Renwick's Norman plan for the new building of the Smithsonian Institution. However, that was not to be the end of the great battle of the architects, for the Board continued to be bombarded by requests for payments, consideration of a wider selection of architects, and other complaints.[9]

The Regents had been beset by negative public opinion and architectural furor. It was in reaction to these experiences that Owen characteristically determined to write a sound, highly detailed argument to silence his critics by force of reason and logic in a defense of the stylistic decisions made by the Building Committee. On February 5th of 1847, the resolution of the 30th of November to publish the designs and particulars of the Smithsonian Building was amended to authorize the publication of an illustrated treatise to be entitled *Hints on Public Architecture*.

With the first chapter Owen sounded a call for the development of an American style of public architecture faithful to the past, but responsive to contemporary requirements. Owen ascribed character to architectural elements. In the style of Archibald Alison, the Scot aesthetician of associationism, he defined good architecture (in chapter II) as being "truthful" and, in chapter after chapter, specific examples of ancient and medieval ar-

[8]Isaiah Rogers, *Diary of 1847*, January 1 entry, transcribed by Denys Peter Myers, p. 550, original in Avery Library, Columbia University. Also in Rhees, *Journals*, "Journals of . . . Regents," December 21, 1846, p. 18. Hilliard told LeBrun of Philadelphia in an exchange reported to the Board that anyone could enter designs up to the cutoff date of December 25.

[9]Rhees, *Journals*, "Journal of Proceedings of the Board of Regents," January 30, 1847, pp. 20–31.

chitecture were weighed by this measure. Owen dwelt on the unsuitability of the Neoclassic style which dominated American public architecture in the early nineteenth century, condemning its "air of over-pretention and unappropriateness" (p. 59).[10] His argument for the Gothic was phrased in terms more human than material:

> I like its truth, its candor, its boldness. I like its lofty character, its aspiring lines. I like the independence with which it has shaken off the shackles of formal rules . . . the endless variety of character in its expressions (p. 63).

Behind Owen's argument lay a hidden agenda. Both the illustrations of Renwick's "Castle" and the text described a building which embodied Robert Dale Owen's concept of an educational institution for all the people. Influenced by his father's belief in the betterment of society through education, Owen worked for public education in New Harmony, Indianapolis, and Washington. What he failed to create by law, he sought to achieve by architecture. The dreamy spires and cloistered walkways of the Castle call up a romanticized version of an Oxford college. "Nor," he wrote, "do I believe that anyone, of moderately cultivated taste, in looking upon that building would mistake its character or connect it in his mind, with other than a scientific, or collegiate foundation" (p. 85).

Choosing the vocabulary of medieval collegiate architecture, Owen praised the Gothic for practical reasons which sound familiar to twentieth-century ears. Economy of material, facilities for heating, cooling, and fenestration were the modern necessities which were not easily adaptable to the classical formula, but which were readily attainable with the early Gothic style (or late Norman as he called it). He deprecated the popular Roman and Renaissance styles for betraying the basic principle "that external form should be the faithful interpreter of internal purpose" (p. 48).

Discussion of material and costs was one of the original intentions of the Regents in resolving to publish this book. Toward the end of the book, technical data—comparative cost and specifications—were used by Owen to support his contention that this chosen admixture of Norman Romanesque and Early Gothic would be less costly a style than Neoclassical. This theme, too, was predetermined by Owen before the deliberations of the Building Committee or

---

[10]References to passages in *Hints* will be cited thus in the text, (p. 59).

the choice of Renwick's design. "I have adopted, as suggested, the Norman style of architecture," David Dale had written in 1845. "Of all ornamental styles, the Norman, in its various modifications, is the most economical, and the best amidst the introduction of all sorts of conveniences."[11] The selection of a building material was concluded after lengthy consideration and technical tests of materials ranging widely in color and qualities. The results of this study of materials appeared in *Hints* as the appendix without mention that the search for a building stone was carried out under the active direction of David Dale Owen.

Living in the intensely intellectual atmosphere of New Harmony, both Robert Dale Owen and David Dale Owen were aware of the large number of works on architectural history appearing in the late 1830s and 1840s, beginning with Thomas Rickman's *Outline of Architecture* and continuing through the efforts of sensitive amateurs such as William Whewell and Thomas Hope. In the tradition of the essayist, Owen borrowed the arguments of contemporary writers, but added his own observations. The didactic message was his own, the arguments and illustrations come from a catholic selection—sources in three languages ranging from technical essays to elaborate picture books. As a result, this book is a distinctively personal précis of some of the cultural attitudes of the time.

Even before the appointments of Joseph Henry as Secretary and Charles Jewett as Librarian, the Smithsonian purchased a significant number of books, all of them on architectural subjects. It could be assumed, from Robert Dale Owen's prominent position as member of the Executive Committee and of the Building Committee, that this order was placed on his responsibility. In fact, evidence has come to light to confirm this. A copy of John Henry Parker's *Glossary of Architecture* was discovered in the Library of Congress, bearing on its flyleaf the inscription in Robert Dale Owen's handwriting, "This is the first book purchased for the Institution." The comment is signed "R.D.O."

Clearly, Owen applied himself to a serious review of contemporary literature on the subject of architecture. He ordered, on November 24th, twenty-two assorted volumes, including all five volumes of Loudon's *Architectural Magazine*, three works by Pugin, one by LeKeux, Rickman's *Architecture*,

[11]David Dale Owen to Robert Dale Owen, New Harmony, October 20, 1845, in "Correspondence" and in Arnot, *Animadversions*, p. 8.

Whewell's *Essay on German Churches*, two volumes by Britton, and an analytical index to Hope.[12] It should be noted that these works were ordered more than a month before any mention was made of publishing even a small volume on the subject of the Building Committee's deliberations. Many of the books on this list, however, provided substantive material for comments found in *Hints on Public Architecture*. The following figure prominently in the book: Loudon's *Architectural Magazine*, Pugin's *Gothic Architecture*, and Pugin's *Normandy*, Caveler's *Gothic Architecture*, Rickman's *Architecture*, Whewell on *German Churches*, Britton's *Cathedral Antiquities* and *Architectural Antiquities*, Moller's *Denkmaller*, *Le Moyen Age Pittoresque* and *Le Moyen Age Monumental*, Gailhabaud's *Ancient and Modern Architecture*, Wheale's *Quarterly Papers on Architecture*, and Hope's *Historical Essay*. Other references cited include Cotman's *Architectural Antiquities of Normandy*, Wilkin's edition of Vitruvius' *On Architecture*, Wood's *Ruins of Palmyra*, Palladio, and William Kent's *The Designs of Inigo Jones*.

By examining the source of the illustrations and footnotes of this book we can see that Owen was seriously concerned with preparing himself to deal knowledgeably with the question of this architectural decision. He determined to read widely, and supplemented his reading with travel. The use of the books cited above in *Hints* shows that Owen had read and used material from the library purchased for the Institution. His trips to Boston, Philadelphia, Trenton, New York and Cincinnati reveal him taking a bold step by placing in equal consideration with the monuments of the past and of Europe those more recent and more native to this country. It would seem that consideration of an appropriate public architecture for the American nation was in Owen's mind from the beginning of this undertaking. Consistently, this was his concern in writing *Hints on Public Architecture*.

The rising tide of nationalism of the 1840s which found expression in territorial expansion and in political change was a stimulus to seek new forms of architectural expression. As a legislator, Owen had participated in this change. As a social reformer based in the forward-looking community of New Harmony, he had been an advocate for it. Now he turned his attention to the question of its expression in a national public architecture. He defined the national character as having purity, vigor, flexibility, independence, breadth,

[12]Rhees, *Documents*, p. 343.

and practical economy. These characteristics he translated into a medieval style of architecture with flexible layout, picturesque silhouette, and bold use of native materials (pp. 5–9). In the pages of this book he marshalled all of the learned sources he had read and the experiences of his work on the Building Committee to justify his conviction.

To the town of New Harmony, the State of Indiana, and the nation which he adopted by choice, Robert Dale Owen contributed a diversified heritage of social concern. In *Hints on Public Architecture* he has left us an earnest and deeply personal contribution to the American cultural heritage. There is a maverick charm about this essay not present in more sophisticated architectural writing. This is a work which remains delightfully readable and thought-provoking for the modern reader.

Washington, D.C.
January, 1978

CYNTHIA R. FIELD
Research Associate
for Architectural History
Smithsonian Institution

MAIN ENTRANCE, NORTH FRONT, SMITHSONIAN INSTITUTION.

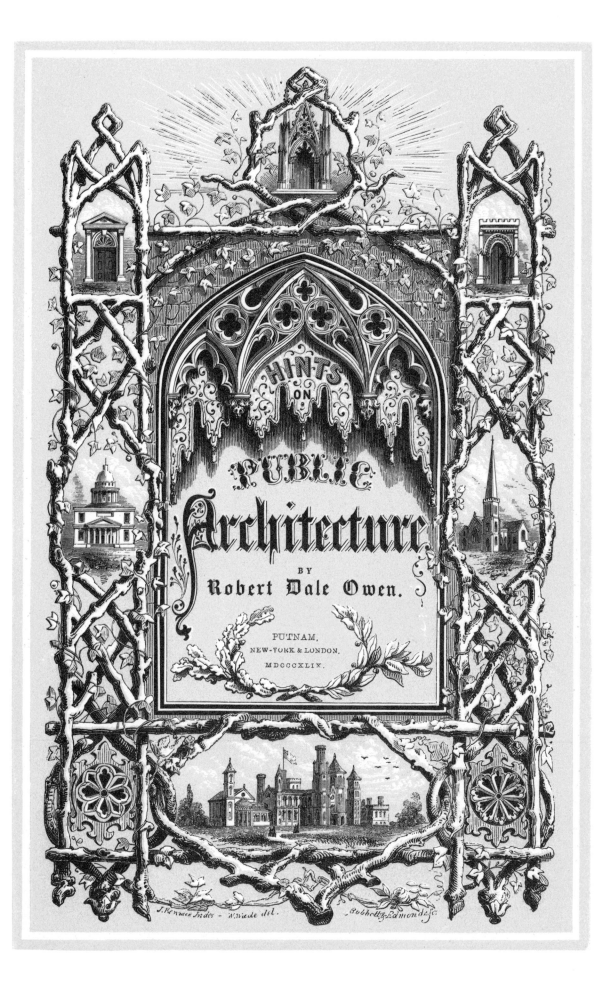

HINTS
ON

PUBLIC

Architecture

BY
Robert Dale Owen.

PUTNAM,
NEW-YORK & LONDON.
MDCCCXLIX.

HINTS

ON

PUBLIC ARCHITECTURE,

CONTAINING, AMONG OTHER ILLUSTRATIONS,

VIEWS AND PLANS OF THE SMITHSONIAN INSTITUTION:

TOGETHER WITH AN

APPENDIX RELATIVE TO BUILDING MATERIALS.

PREPARED, ON BEHALF OF THE BUILDING COMMITTEE OF THE SMITHSONIAN INSTITUTION,

BY

ROBERT DALE OWEN,

CHAIRMAN OF THE COMMITTEE.

NEW-YORK:

GEORGE P. PUTNAM, 155 BROADWAY,
AND 142 STRAND, LONDON.

1849.

Entered according to Act of Congress, in the year 1849, by

GEORGE P. PUTNAM,

In the Clerk's Office of the District Court, for the Southern District of New York.

Typography by E. O. JENKINS.   Presswork by C. A. ALVORD.

INTRODUCTORY NOTICE,

BY THE BUILDING COMMITTEE OF THE SMITHSONIAN INSTITUTION.

THE circumstances which gave rise to the present volume are mentioned in the Preface. But it is, notwithstanding, deemed proper for the Building Committee here to state, that this work is put forth, not by the Smithsonian Institution as one of their series of "Smithsonian Contributions to Knowledge," but by the Building Committee of that Institution, under a resolution of the Board of Regents adopted on the 5th of February, 1847, authorizing the Committee to publish, in such form as they might deem most appropriate, a brief treatise on Public Architecture.

The manuscript was submitted by the Building Committee to gentlemen in whose taste and judgment they place confidence, namely, to President Everett, of Cambridge, Massachusetts, to Mr. Gouverneur Kemble, of New York, and to Judge Kane of Philadelphia; and these gentlemen, without endorsing all the opinions therein set forth, (and for which, in truth, an individual author alone can be responsible,) concur in bearing testimony to the value of the treatise, and in recommending its publication, as shown by the following extracts from their respective letters:

EXTRACT OF A LETTER FROM PRESIDENT EVERETT, DATED CAMBRIDGE, DEC. 4, 1848.

"If it be not going beyond my province, I would recommend the publication of the manuscript, not as a 'Smithsonian Contribution to Knowledge,' but in the usual form in which the Reports of Committees are published. In this form I think it will be regarded as an ingenious, spirited and valuable performance, creditable to the talents and research of the Author."

EXTRACT OF A LETTER FROM GOUVERNEUR KEMBLE, ESQ., DATED COLD SPRING, NEW YORK, DECEMBER 6, 1848.

"I consider that the 'Hints on Architecture' would be highly creditable to the Institution, as the work of one of its members, a man of talents and of cultivated taste; and although I should hesitate in giving its sanction to everything that they contain, I would recommend its publication with the name of the Author."

EXTRACT OF A LETTER FROM JUDGE J. K. KANE, DATED PHILADELPHIA, DEC. 20, 1848.

" Mr. Owen's paper, in its researches and tone, is altogether scholarlike; and it is certainly among the most polished and *readable* of the essays I have met with on the subject. I recommend that it be published by the Institution; and if it be, they will, I think, have done good by aiding in the diffusion of just views and liberal taste."

PREFACE.

In the difficulties which presented themselves to the Building Committee of the Smithsonian Institution, when they first entered on the task assigned them, this Treatise had its origin. They now give to the Public that which they would themselves have rejoiced to find in condensed form and language divested of technicalities, and which, not thus finding, they had to seek through numerous volumes and under a load of professional detail.

To the improvement of Architecture are essential, not only genius and skill in the artist who designs, but discrimination in the tribunal to which his designs are submitted. But while much talent and industry have been expended on treatises suited to the wants of the professional student, few works have been prepared having for special object to enlighten the judgment and form the taste of those who are appointed to sit in judgment on the result of his labors, and who have power to transfer, from paper to reality, the creations of his brain.

Such considerations induced the Executive Board of the Institution, under whose auspices the present volume appears, to modify their first intention in the premises; which was, merely to gratify the proper curiosity of the Public in regard to the plan and style of Architecture selected for their building, and to the reasons which governed them in that selection. They have judged it useful and conducive to the increase and diffusion of knowledge in an important department of Art, to go beyond their original purpose, and to authorize the Committee having the erection of that building specially in charge, to cast together, in connected form, such hints in regard to Public Architecture, the merit and cost of its various manners, and the facility of adapting each to modern purposes, as were gathered during investigations and researches first undertaken for an object more restricted and specific.

While the Committee offer the result of these researches not so much to the Profession as to the Public, and to public bodies (as Vestries, Building Committees and the like) charged with duties similar to their own, they indulge the hope, that the architect also may find occasional subject for inquiry and material for thought. Much of what is here written must be familiar to every well-read student; there will occur to him the very sources whence it is derived: but a portion of the pages which follow are of a character less commonplace. A strict recurrence to first principles in Art, a distinct recognition of the conditions, not transitory and conventional, but changeless and inherent, that go to stamp upon architectural creations purity of manner and excellence of composition; these are matters wholly omitted in many works on Architecture, and but slightly glanced at in others. It may not be without its use to the Profession, to withdraw their thoughts, for a moment, from the routine of architectural codes set up by various schools as law and doctrine, and bestow them on the deeper sources whence these laws were derived; on the *leges legum*, to use Bacon's phrase; for thus they will penetrate to causes, not gather up a mere bundle of results. " The mindless copyist studies Rafaelle, not what Rafaelle studied."

Purity of style in Architecture is a point of progress not to be suddenly reached. In a new country especially, in which the necessary and the strictly useful properly have precedence, refinement in art is commonly of tardy and gradual growth. There is usually a period of transition, during which the wish to excel precedes, at some distance, the perception of the means of excellence. Money is expended, even lavishly, to obtain the rich, the showy, the commonplace. But this period of transition may be shortened. The progress in Painting and Sculpture, which, in other lands, has been the slow growth of centuries, has been hastened, in our country, thanks to the genius of a few self-taught men, beyond all former precedent. To stimulate genius in a kindred branch of art; to supply suggestions, which may call off from devious paths, and indicate, to the student, the true line of progress; and thus to aid in abridging that season of experiment and of failure in which the glittering is preferred to the chaste, and the gaudy is mistaken for the beautiful; are objects of no light importance. In such considerations may be found the motive and the purpose of the following pages.

The Committee entrusted to its Chairman their immediate preparation. In discharging the duty assigned him, he has availed himself freely of the labors of former writers; acknowledging his authority, whenever he has literally adopted the sentiment of another ; but, in many instances, unavoidably selecting and repeating, from that literary storehouse of common property of which every art has its own, much that has been put forth, once and again, by others before him. He has frequently fallen into the same train of thought which runs through Thomas Hope's well-known Historical Essay; than which few more valuable works on Architecture have ever appeared, in our own or in any other language.

To several gentlemen, to whose discriminating criticism the manuscript of the work has been submitted—to some, by himself; to others, at the instance of the Committee—the Author owes an acknowledgment for important emendations and valuable suggestions; the more important and valuable to him, because his task was undertaken without the aid of that guiding experience, which professional training and the actual practice of construction alone can give.

Of the illustrations which enrich his work, he may be allowed to say, that he regards them as creditable to American art. A portion of these are from original designs; but where examples of ancient Architecture, not found on our Continent, are given, these, from the necessity of the case, are copied from illustrations in European works; the source whence each is derived being, in every case, acknowledged. There was no alternative but to pursue this course, or else to send a draughtsman, at an expense which the object would not justify, to the various countries of Europe and Asia where the originals are found.

For many of the sketches that were placed in the engraver's hands, as well as for efficient aid in preparing the text of the present treatise, he is indebted to the gentleman whose design was adopted for the Smithsonian Institution building; a structure frequently alluded to in the pages which follow; and which may be said to furnish, as to many of the observations there set forth, both text and commentary.

R. D. O.

March, 1849.

CONTENTS.

CHAPTER I.

TOUCHING SOME GENERAL CONDITIONS OF EXCELLENCE IN ARCHITECTURE.

CHAPTER II.

CONCERNING SOME CONDITIONS OF PURITY IN STYLE.

CHAPTER III.

CONCERNING THE TWO GREAT DIVISIONS OF MANNER IN ARCHITECTURE.

CHAPTER IV.

ADAPTATION OF POST AND LINTEL ARCHITECTURE TO MODERN PURPOSES.

CHAPTER V.

OF HYBRID ARCHITECTURE.

CHAPTER VI.

OF ARCH ARCHITECTURE.

CHAPTER VII.

OF ANACHRONISMS IN ARCHITECTURE.

CHAPTER VIII.

RELATIVE TO THE COMPARATIVE COST OF THE ARCH AND POST AND LINTEL MANNERS.

LIST OF ILLUSTRATIONS.

PLATES.

WOOD-CUTS

INCORPORATED IN THE TEXT.

HINTS ON PUBLIC ARCHITECTURE.

HINTS ON ARCHITECTURE.

CHAPTER I.

TOUCHING SOME GENERAL CONDITIONS OF EXCELLENCE IN ARCHITECTURE.

" Architecture is essentially an art of direct utility ; its productions must be ruled by certain conditions, not of mere resemblance, but of fitness. The conditions by which their merits are to be estimated, are not so much retrospective as prospective."

Hope's Historical Essay.

THERE is this difference between the arts of Architecture and Sculpture, that excellence in the latter is universal and of no age; while justly to judge the merits of the former, considerations of time and place, of custom and climate, must come into view. The Apollo of the Vatican is the type, not of the Greek of two thousand years ago, but of human majesty. Success in such a creation, was success for all nations and for all time. That noble statue is as much in place here, in our modern world, with all the progressive changes which twenty centuries have seen, and all the accumulated inventions and improvements which these centuries have left behind them, as it was at Antium, when, in its first beauty, it adorned the villa of a tyrant.

But for Architecture, strictly an art of utility, there is no abstract excellence, because there is no universal fitness. It is an art properly, even necessarily, modified by the progress of the world and the successive wants and habits and sentiments of successive generations. And, as it is an art of which the essential purpose is, to furnish shelter from the elements, its fitting productions must vary, like those of the field or the forest, from climate to climate. The cool and open colonnades that seem indigenous under the ardent sun and bright skies of Greece, can with as little propriety be transplanted to Lapland, there to be reared amid snows and tempests, as might her olives or her orange groves.

With varying material, too, must vary the phases of architectural character. That marble of Carrara, of which the Apollo is one of the earliest specimens, is commonly used, even to-day, by sculptors throughout the civilized world.   But the materials for building are too ponderous to justify, in a general way, distant transportation.   They are usually sought in the immediate vicinity, and are found, now in the clay of the valley, now in the hillside quarry, and again, of more perishable character, in the forest tree.   Of late years a rival material, from the mine, seems encroaching on these; and the next generation may see, arising on our Continent, villages, or it may be cities, of iron.   But brick and stone and wood tend, respectively, to give to the buildings of which they are the chief components, a distinctive character; and who shall say what further changes may be wrought, if, hereafter, in rich mineral districts, the iron mine supersede the quarry ?

There is yet another element which contributes to stamp on Architecture its character of change and progress.   The chisel of Chantry, or Canova, or Powers, is but the same simple tool, which, in the hands of Phidias, embodied poetry in marble; and the modern sculptor works out his conception by the same slow and tedious process resorted to by his predecessors of the olden time.   But with the advance of mathematical knowledge, and the increase of mechanical skill, changes of the most radical character have been wrought in Architecture.   The discovery and employment of the arch alone, produced, in its ultimate results, a complete revolution in the art.

It is among the conditions of a true Architecture, then, that it mould itself to the wants and the domestic habits and the public customs and the political institutions and the religious sentiment of its country and its age; that it assort with the materials at hand, submitting to modifications as new materials present themselves; and that it avail itself, from time to time, of the various aids which mathematical and mechanical and chemical science offer, for its convenience and advancement.

It results from these considerations, that an Architecture of another age and another country may be eminently deserving our admiration, not only as a work of art, but as proper and fitting, at the time and in the place it arose, and yet be wholly unworthy of imitation, at this day, among us.   Some of its forms, a portion of its details, may furnish to us valuable models, or, at least, useful subjects of study; but, as a whole, it may neither adapt itself to the exigencies of our times, nor comport with the inclemency of our seasons.   Some of its characteristics may be only rude expedients to evade difficulties, which the mechanical skill of modern science has long since overcome.

In our republican land, we need no time-defying pyramids, devised, as those of Egypt probably were, to occupy and keep quiet an indolent people.   In a country emphatically of change and of progress, to what purpose the Cyclopean massiveness of ancient Indian and Egyptian piles, modelled after stupendous excavations, more ancient yet, cut in the solid rock; or even of that Temple of the Sun at Baalbec with blocks of stone in its basement, weighing a thousand tons apiece, and of which a single one would stretch across the entire front of a spacious modern edifice?*

The Kalaisa, Ellora. †

* Of three stones found in the base of the Temple of the Sun at Baalbec, (situated nearly midway between Damascus and Tripoli,) the collective length is *one hundred and ninety-nine feet*; the depth of each from back to front, exclusive of a bold and rich cornice, ten feet five inches; and the height thirteen feet.

Mr. Wood, who has published beautiful illustrations of the ruins of Palmyra and of Baalbec, found, in a freestone quarry not far from the city wall, and from which the above colossal blocks were taken, another of dimensions still greater. It measured *seventy* feet in length, fourteen in breadth, and fourteen and a half in height. Its weight, taking the average density of freestone, must have been upwards of eleven hundred tons.

† Ellora is a village of Hindostan, in the province of Aurungabad. Some of its excavations are subter-

What should we do, in our utilitarian age, with religious structures so vast, that above them might spring up, as above the temples of Luxor, a village, with its inhabitants?* Or how would it suit our matter-of-fact country to see constructed, in her cities, shambles which, like those of Nero, might be mistaken for palaces? With what object should we construct an amphitheatre, enclosing, as that of Vespasian did, its half dozen acres, and seating its hundred thousand spectators, since, now-a-days, it is not the custom to set on gladiators, nor even wild beasts, to slaughter each other? Who, even, would erect, and for what purpose should we occupy, a republican St. Peter's, the copy of that, to complete the erection of which the Roman pontiff laid all Christendom under contribution? The day of mere imposing ceremony is gone by. Churches, among us, are used to speak and to hear in; and their purpose restricts their dimensions. But what human voice can fill those splendid monuments of skill and taste, left behind by a wonderful fraternity, the cathedrals of Continental Europe? that of Antwerp, for example, with its treble aisles? or that of Cologne, capable of receiving and sheltering, under the roof of its magnificent nave, the tallest spires, with a few individual exceptions, to be found throughout our entire country?†

We *have* sought to rival the temples of Greece. A school for penniless orphans, endowed by the wealth of a plain man, has assumed a form of classic grandeur, that emulates, if at somewhat remote distance, even the pride of Athens, that temple of Jupiter Olympius, with its Corinthian columns of Pentelic marble, which demanded,

---

raneous and some are isolated; among the most remarkable of the latter is the Kalaisa, a monument dedicated to Siva, of which a portion is here figured, from Gailhabaud's "Ancient and Modern Architecture." The whole of its buildings, together with the area on which they stand, are hewn out of the living rock and completely detached from the mountain. It has the appearance of an edifice built stone by stone, yet the entire mass consists of one unjointed block, and is strictly entitled to the epithet *monolithic*.

These excavations, in their greatest length, from the foot of the hill, are four hundred and one feet; and they have a breadth varying from one hundred and forty to one hundred and eighty-five feet. Indian traditions give them an antiquity of nearly eight thousand years; but modern writers incline to the opinion that to date them back two thousand years is a more reasonable calculation.

* "The temples of Luxor bear an Arab village."—*Hope's Essay, Note to p.* 13. The expression, however, must be received in a restricted sense. The character of Egyptian Architecture, with its hypæthral areas, prolonged walls and tower-like pylons, precludes the idea of smaller habitations perched upon its temples. Over portions of these vast ruins the sand has drifted; and upon this, groups of Arab huts have been erected, and are occupied, I believe, at the present day.

Luxor is one of four villages, now found on the site of ancient Thebes. Its temples stand on the banks of the Nile. Belzoni's impressions, on first beholding the remains of that marvellous city, to which Homer, in scarcely hyperbolical phrase, applied the epithet *hundred-gated*, are vividly given:

"It appeared to me like entering a city of giants, who, after a long conflict, had been all destroyed, leaving the ruins of their various temples as the only proofs of their former existence."

There is in Carnac, another of these villages, a hall whose roof, of flat stones, is sustained by more than a hundred and thirty pillars; some twenty-six feet and others *thirty-four* feet in circumference.

† The nave of Cologne Cathedral is one hundred and eighty feet high.

for its completion, the resources of eight centuries.*   Whether such rivalry be wise, and how far the forms of the Grecian model adapt themselves to the wants of a later age, of a more northern climate, and of a more advanced civilization, are questions to which, in the course of this brief treatise, there may be occasion to revert.

If it should appear that none of these ancient manners may fittingly be adopted, let us not too deeply regret that the architectural magnificence of the Past may forever remain unequalled in the Future.   That treasure which the Egyptians lavished on the sepulture of the dead, we are content to appropriate, with more wisdom surely, to the comforts of the living.   Those sums which were expended, in a feudal age, to rear, throughout Europe, embattled fortresses, were they not spent in rivetting the chains of the serf?   When the eye of some citizen of this New World, as he descends the Rhine, rests on the castellated heights, of which the dark masses and picturesque outline so greatly add to the romantic beauty of that noble stream, shall he turn with a sigh to reflect, that *his* country presents no remains of such imposing grandeur?   Let him rather call to mind, that these lordly castles, with all their poetical accesso-

---

* The temple of Jupiter Olympius (at Athens, not to be confounded with that, erected to the same deity, at Agrigentum, and celebrated for its colossal Atlantes,) was a *dipteros;* that is, the cell was surrounded by a double row of columns.   These columns were about six feet and a half in diameter and nearly sixty feet high ; fluted, of Pentelic marble, with beautiful Corinthian capitals and Attic bases.

The editor of Stuart's well-known work on Athens, calls it "the largest and most sumptuous of all the temples of ancient Hellas ;" its dimensions being, as nearly as can be now ascertained, one hundred and sixty-seven feet in front, and three hundred and seventy-two feet in length, from east to west.

Stuart's restored plan of this temple shows four rows of ten columns each in the portico, and the same in the posticum. (See ground-plan, given in the fourth chapter of this work.)

The Girard College, measured to the edge of the outer steps, is about one hundred and fifty-nine feet by two hundred and eighteen.   Its cella is one hundred and eleven feet by one hundred and sixty-nine, surrounded by a single colonnade ; the columns of American marble, fluted ; the order, Grecian Corinthian ; copied, I believe, with some modifications, from the choragic monument of Lysicrates. The columns are six feet in diameter, fifty-five feet in height, and thirty-four in number ; eight on each end and eleven on each side.   The effect of this magnificent and imposing temple elevation is marred by the disproportionate breadth as compared to the length of the edifice.   In reference to this matter, the Architect (Mr. Walter) says, in his final Report : "I should undoubtedly have made the flanks at least four columns more in length ; but the length, breadth and height of the cella having been established by Mr. Girard in his will, there was no alternative left but to make the cella according to the specified

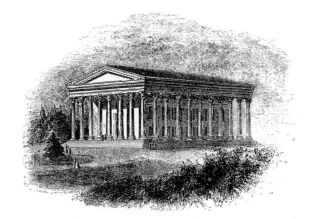

Girard College, Philadelphia.

dimensions, and adapt the peristyle to it as best I might, without regarding the relative proportion between the front and flanks."

ries of moat and bastion, of battlement and tower, were once but the strong-holds of titled robbers, the receptacles of plunder, the scenes of extortion and cruelty and rapine. They cursed, while they adorned, the country. The absence, even, of enduring material for building, might, in those days of baronial misrule, have been a political blessing. Laing, an intelligent traveller, in his " Journal of a Residence in Norway," alluding to the fact that the stone of the country, though abundant, was considered, from its hardness and irregular forms, too expensive a building material, shrewdly enough regards the temporary character thence imparted to Norwegian architecture as one among the causes that have obstructed, in that land, the growth of feudal authority. " Wood," he says, " was the material at all times, for all classes of dwellings, from the palace of the monarch to the peasant's hut. It was, everywhere, abundant and cheap. This circumstance has been more important than may at first appear, in the destinies of the country. The chieftains or nobility had no strong-holds in which they could secure themselves and their retainers. When at variance with a more powerful neighbor, or with their sovereign, they, with their adherents, could only retire to their ships."

We need, it is true, no such precaution here, against the encroachment of marauding nobles; but neither do we require those fortress-dwellings, in which the Suzerain of the Middle Ages defied alike the commands of a feeble sovereign, and the complaints of an oppressed peasantry.

Let us not, then, lament the paucity in our land, of memorials of the Past, but rather look on to our Future. If no school of Architecture that has hitherto prevailed, neither the Egyptian, with its sepulchral grandeur, nor the Grecian, with its broad, transverse shadows and its quiet repose, nor the ornate and aspiring Gothic, may, as as a whole, serve as a suitable model for us, now in this nineteenth century and here on this North American Continent, then the inquiry presents itself, may we not hope to see spring up in our midst, a school of our own; assimilated, more or less, to one or other of the old manners; yet asserting its privilege to originate as well as to adopt; not only to select, here and there, without challenge or charge of anachronism, whatever old forms may appropriately clothe the various interiors, upon which domestic convenience or public necessities shall have stamped shape and arrangement and dimensions; but also, when old forms fail, to do, what architects of true genius in all ages have done, to create, for new internal combinations, their suitable exterior; their own characteristic phase of expression, and fitting style of decoration.

This is no new idea. One who devoted a lifetime to the study of the art; who spent eight years of travel throughout most of the nations of the civilized world in architectural research; after having looked upon all that Egyptian and Grecian and Italian and Moorish and Persian and Gothic artists have left of grandest or most beautiful, to rouse our wonder or claim our admiration; the late Thomas Hope closes his celebrated Historical Essay with the following paragraph:

"No one seems yet to have conceived the wish or idea of only borrowing of every former style of Architecture, whatever it might present of useful or ornamental, of scientific or tasteful; of adding thereto whatever other new dispositions or forms might afford conveniences or elegancies not yet possessed; of making the new discoveries, the new conquests, of natural productions unknown to former ages, the models of new imitations more beautiful and more varied; and thus of composing an Architecture which, born in our country, grown on our soil, and in harmony with our climate, institutions and habits, at once elegant, appropriate and original, shall truly deserve the appellation of '*our own.*'"

If such a task seem beset with difficulty; if it demand rare genius, absolute devotion; if, fitly to accomplish it, there lack untiring research, penetrating to the very spirit of the past; a judgment that early prepossessions cannot bribe, nor latent prejudices influence; a fancy fertile without exuberance; resource to originate and taste to combine; still, there is no cause for despair. How much, in the departments of painting and sculpture, has our young country already achieved! Why, in a branch more strictly utilitarian, should we doubt the purity, or the vigor, of her creative powers?

Let us bear in mind, however, that towards national advancement in this, as in every other department of art, not alone the artists who labor, but we also, the public for whom they labor, have a great duty to perform. Veneration for the past sometimes degenerates into injustice to the present. Our eyes, fastened upon the brilliant beacons that shine upon us from out the obscurity of the olden time, may remain blind to lights as pure and radiant, that have birth in our own day and our own land, and that need but the genial breath of encouraging commendation to fan them into brightness and power. It has been well said by an eloquent modern writer,* that "if honor be for the dead, gratitude can only be for the living." And it is a melancholy reflection, how much of true genius, that might have outshone all the brilliancy of the past, may have been checked by careless indifference and quenched by cold neglect.

---

* The author of "Modern Painters." The whole passage is one of singular beauty and truth. After alluding to that regret, natural to the human mind, when some one whom in life we have not sufficiently prized and loved is removed by the hand of death beyond the reach of all atoning kindness, the writer adds: "But the lesson which men receive as individuals, they do not learn as nations. Again and again they have seen their noblest descend into the grave, and have thought it enough to garland the tombstone when they had not crowned the brow, and to pay the honor to the ashes which they had denied to the spirit. Let it not displease them, that they are bidden, amidst the tumult and the dazzle of their busy life, to listen for the few voices, and watch for the few lamps, which God has toned and lighted to charm and to guide them; that they may not learn their sweetness by their silence, nor their light by their decay."—*Introduction*, p. 7.

There are certain conditions which it is safe to set down as essential, in any style of Architecture that shall justly obtain, in our republic, the character of national.

It must possess a certain flexibility. Its external forms must not control and dictate its internal adaptations, but must yield and lend itself to these. That freedom, the vital principle of our political system, must breathe its spirit also over our architectural code. There must be no forced, inexorable correspondence of parts; no Procrustean regularity, which to invade, no matter how just the cause, is to be ruled high treason against the art. The unity of the whole must not be judged to be violated by the independent variety of its parts. We must discard our lingering predilections for that old system, little suited either to the genius or the wants of our land, in which

> " Grove nods to grove, each alley has its brother,
> And half the terrace just reflects the other."

The great extent of our country and the consequent variety of its climate in sections remote from each other, must alone, if no other cause existed, forbid complete uniformity of manner. The Grecian pediment has its fixed proportions, widely to depart from which is forbidden by classic rule. But, in our Architecture, the pitch of roof must not be prescribed. It will be comparatively flat in the climate, almost tropical, of Florida, where snow is a seven years' marvel. It will become more pointed as it approaches the Canadian frontier; because a sharp roof is necessary to resist and discard the superincumbent weight of the heavy snows of Maine. Moller, in his "Denkmähler der Deutchen Baukunst," in discussing that often mooted point, the circumstances which, about the middle of the twelfth century, caused, throughout Germany and other countries, the substitution of the pointed Gothic for the semi-circular arch of Lombardy, attributes that sudden and wide-spreading change of style to the fact, that, as Architecture travelled northward, and as the high, northern gable replaced the low, southern roof, there was required, in order that the rest of the building might harmonize with that altered feature, a higher and sharper arch than the half circle.*

Our national Architecture must not be of elaborate or expensive style. In a country in which it is a recognized principle, that its people shall not be taxed beyond the necessary expenses of government, reasonable economy in regard to its public buildings is, in the strictest sense, a duty.

It follows, that, in our Architecture, we should trust for effect rather to justness of

---

* "Das hohe, nördliche Dach verdrängte den flachen, südlichen Giebel, und diese Einführung des hohen Dachgiebels zog, wenn die übrigen Theile des Gebaudes hiermit in Uebereinstimmung seyn sollten, den Gebrauch des Spitzbogens, statt des Halbkreises, nach sich."—*Moller's Denkmähler*, vol. i, p. 7.

proportion, to graceful outline, to skillful grouping and artistical management of masses, than to gorgeous ornament or costly decoration. Not only must we avoid such glaring aberrations from good taste, as those recorded and reprobated by Pliny* and Seneca† and Vitruvius, the staining even of the richest marbles with additional spots of various hues to add to their brilliancy; but the more legitimate adornments of rich carvings, delicate tracery, glowing arabesques, must enter, if at all, but sparingly into our republican style. In all its accessories, whatever entails heavy expense should be avoided. Smoothly to dress the external face of a building, for example, adds largely to its cost. It is, therefore, no inconsiderable item in favor of a style, if, like the Norman or Gothic, it harmonize with a rough character of finish.‡

The natural productions of our country may sometimes advantageously furnish

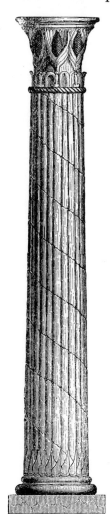

original materials for architectural ornament. Our maize leaf is not less graceful in form than the lotus of Egypt or the acanthus of Greece; and the pillars in the lower vestibule of the Senate entrance to the Capitol, (their clustered shafts representing a bundle of reeds or stalks of Indian corn, and their capitals composed of the ear and leaf of the same plant,) must be regarded as a happy inspiration of Latrobe's.§ Pillars of similar character will

* Lib. xxxv, c. i. It seems to be now very generally conceded, that, long before the reign of Claudius, (to which Pliny, in the above passage, ascribes the commencement of painting marble,) even in the purest period of Grecian art, a portion of the ornaments on the entablature and elsewhere, in marble temples, were painted or stained or gilt. This is very much at variance with the usual ideas, which base the essential character and excellencies of the Grecian school solely on beauty of form and proportion, and on the unaided effect of light and shade. Those who desire to examine for themselves the evidences of ancient Polychromy may consult Hittorff in his "Architecture Polychrôme des Grecs:" also Dr. Kugler's work, "Ueber die Polychromie der Griechischen Architektur und Sculptur und ihre Grenzen."

† Lib x, c. xxxvi. 4.

‡ The Smithsonian building supplies an example of a rough finish, according well with the character of its architecture. To have given it a smooth exterior, like that of the General Post Office, or so elaborate a finish as that adopted for Trinity Church, New York, would have added some fourteen or fifteen thousand dollars to the cost of the structure.

When freestone of good quality is the building material, a rough finish has this further advantage, that the slight encroachments which, in the lapse of years, time and the elements make on its surface, but tend to smooth its asperities and thus improve its appearance; while, on a surface already smooth, the effect of the least encroachment is, in a measure, to deface and disfigure.

Capitol, Washington.

§ The original design of the Capitol of the United States was partly by Dr. William Thornton, and partly by Mr. B. H. Latrobe; and the building was completed under the superintendence of Mr. C. Bulfinch, as architect, in 1830. The corner-stone was laid by General Washington, September 18, 1793. The maize pillars above referred to were Mr. Latrobe's

be introduced in the principal porch of the Smith-sonian building. The leaf and the blossom of the tobacco plant, another great staple of our country, have supplied details, less happy however, in the columns of the circular vestibule between the Ro-tunda and the Senate Chamber.

Perhaps the chief difficulty he will have to encoun-ter who shall seek to supply to this New World an Architecture of its own, will be to preserve the rare and happy medium between too much and too little of imitation; to maintain that equable candor of judgment which passion cannot disturb nor prejudice lead astray; which neither blindly venerates the old, because it is old, nor anxiously strains after the new, for the mere sake of novelty. But the same difficulty exists in all sublunary pursuits. One of the most valuable, at once, and of the most rare among human endowments, is a justly balanced judgment.

Base and Capital.

design; and it is said they attracted the notice, and the commendation, of Thomas Jefferson. To the kindness of Mr. John H. B. Latrobe of Baltimore, son of Mr. Latrobe the elder, I am indebted for the original drawings from which the above cuts (both the entire pillar, and the details of its base and capital) are taken.

Castle of Heidelberg, Rhine.

CHAPTER II.

CONCERNING SOME CONDITIONS OF PURITY IN STYLE.

"However poetically art may speak, it should not the less speak truth."

ANONYMOUS.

So long as the architect or the builder rigidly restricts himself, in his designs, to the necessary and the strictly useful; so long as his windows are mere unadorned openings to admit the light and the air, and his doors but a convenient medium of entrance and exit; so long as he remains satisfied with plain brick or painted weather-boarding; if only his proportions be good, and his materials neatly put together, there can be no offence, for there is no pretension. As in the unassuming manners of a blunt, unlettered man, we do not miss that of which we are not reminded. In all countries, but especially in a new and rapidly settling country like ours, a large proportion of edifices, public and private, must retain this purely utilitarian character; and it would be creditable to the good sense of our citizens, if that proportion were even greater than it is. It is something not to fail where we cannot succeed; and there can be no failure where there is no attempt.

But the voice of ambition is enticing. A county court-house must have its spire or its portico; a village church must be distinguished from the secular buildings that surround it; and when we reach our cities, there are banks to be adorned, and insurance offices aspiring after colonnade and pediment; to say nothing of the wants of city corporations, of wealthy colleges, and of religious congregations with means that suffice to reproduce here, on a small scale, the cathedrals of the Old World. And thus the architect, who might otherwise have been content to sit down safely entrenched behind the line of bare utility, is tempted across that boundary into the dangerous domain of taste; sometimes without having very deeply studied the laws of the country into which he enters.

It would be fruitless, even if it were reasonable, to inveigh against the love of ornament. It is inherent in our nature. Like the rest of our passions and propensities, it may be chastened and controlled, but not uprooted; and like them, it may become, under proper discipline, a source of pleasure, both legitimate and improving.

In a commercial country, prosperous as ours, there will always be surplus funds, to be expended on objects not of necessity; and it would be difficult for the severest moralist to explain, why the gratification which gracefulness of structure or beauty of architectural combination, or chaste elegance of decoration, impart to the cultivated mind, should be ascetically denied to it.

Enough, that architectural ornament will be sought for among us, and that money will be appropriated to obtain it. How much better that that money should be spent under the guidance of just taste, than that it should be squandered, to produce the meretricious or the unmeaning!

Such considerations have dictated the few hints here following; and of which the practical application must be left, where it belongs, to the profession.

The same quality which is the foundation of purity of morals is an essential element, also, in purity of architectural style; TRUTH. External form should be the interpreter of internal purpose. That the interpretation be faithful is the first requisite; it is the province of genius, after that, to clothe it with grace and power.

In a pure style, not only must the leading and characteristic forms have birth in specific purpose, but that purpose should be apparent. The imagination should not be misled. Every important feature in a true architecture should have, as it were, self-proclaimed reasons for being what it is.

Common sense suggests, that we should not go in search of forms merely to adorn them. The unreasoning imitator, who penetrates not to the inner principles of a style, is continually violating the maxim, applicable as truly in art as in law, that with the cessation of the cause the effect also should cease. To retain a form, no matter how graceful its outline or how ornamental its parts, in utter disconnection from the true and original purpose which first suggested it, is like clinging to the lifeless corpse after the spirit which animated it has passed away.

We ought to be upon our guard against the influence which the power of association involuntarily exerts upon the mind. Before we imitate even the noblest model, we ought to be assured that the imitation is in place. It is not sufficient servilely to copy the beautiful, in order to obtain it. Beauty is, in a measure, a relative quality. It is a great error to imagine, that what has impressed us as beautiful, in a certain combination, must continue to please, under every combination and in all circumstances. Strike from beauty its propriety, its fitness; let it become unsuitable and unmeaning, and its essence is gone; a showy but worthless mask alone remains.

The low-pitched roof of the Grecian temple, well suited to the southern climate in which it arose, necessarily terminated, at either extremity, in a triangle, of wide base compared to its height; and this gave to Grecian architecture one of its noblest features, the pediment; surmounting, appropriately and beautifully, the entire temple front, with its stately colonnade. But when an architect becomes so enamored of

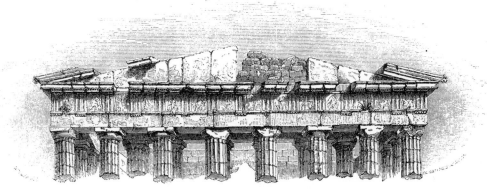

Parthenon, Acropolis, Athens.

this feature as to drag it in where it serves no purpose and exists in no significant relation; perching it, for example, above a portion of the front of a private dwelling, without even a corresponding roof by way of apology for its presence,* and, it may be, with a double or treble row of pillars, erected, one above the other, beneath; or, worse yet, so degraded from its original position and perverted from its true purpose, as to be placed beneath the entablature that ought to underlie and support it; then, no matter how classical may be its cornice, or how elaborate the sculptured enrichments that cover its interior, torn from its proper connection, meaningless and misplaced, it no longer satisfies the discriminating judgment, or commends itself to the cultivated taste.†

So, again, of the classical entablature, the fitting and legitimate support of the pediment above, solid at once and elegant, stretching in level, unbroken line along the summits of the graceful columns that sustain it; its outline, in the distance bold and simple; its details, seen closer at hand, delicate and careful and chaste; who would refuse to the beautiful entablature of the Greeks, placed where the Greeks have placed it, serving the purpose which among the Greeks it served, that tribute of admiration which the creations of true genius command? But when admiration so poorly discriminates, so little discerns the conditions of beauty in architectural feature, as to

---

* Even in some of the finest specimens of Gothic architecture, we occasionally find a sharp-pointed gable set up, usually above the main entrance, between the two front towers, as a mere shield, with no roof behind it. No precedent can justify so meagre an expedient.

† In the temple of Baalbec, the pediment is found set up, by way of ornament, under a projecting portico; where it could not be useful, even to carry off the wet.

On the east front of St. Peter's a heavy attic, rising behind the central pediment and overtopping it, renders it at once misplaced and insignificant.

cut up this entablature into shreds and patches; to mount a mere detached sample of it, high and narrow and isolated, on its solitary column, a mere incumbrance that has no business there; a gratuitous interpolation that is no whit excused, when its summit is made the resting-place of a Norman or Gothic arch, which, *upon* it but not *of* it, looks strange and awkward in the pseudo-classical neighborhood into which it has been thus inconsiderately thrust; when a blind love of the five orders betrays a man into vagaries like these, it avails little that compass and rule have done their best; that Vitruvius can be quoted in support of the form and proportion of every member from abacus to cymatium; the union is still unhappy, because ill-assorted; it is, as some one has fancifully suggested, the mere juxtaposition of two heterogeneous principles, which cannot mix, and therefore yield no issue.*

Numerous are the puerilities to be found in ancient and modern examples, to which this forced impressment of classical features, without regard to purpose or neighborhood, has given occasion. A notable example may be seen by those who visit our seat of government, on entering the large upper room of the Patent Office.†
Immediately opposite the entrance, the Grecian column and entablature are introduced within an arch with which they have no practical connection; the

Patent Office, Washington.

columns, indeed, bearing the entablature, but the entablature supporting nothing, and appearing there for no imaginable purpose except to steady and connect the columns beneath.‡

If there be, in this hybrid style, an instance of worse treatment towards the unfor-

---

* An illustration, from the interior of St. Paul's, New York, is given in Chapter V.

† Justice to the architect who had in charge the erection of this building requires it should here be stated, that this blunder is not his, but an interpolation upon the original design by a Committee, who were probably better acquainted with the Federal Constitution and the rhetorical pillars which Fourth of July orators introduce to support and adorn it, than with the office of those more tangible props upon which Grecian builders imposed their entablature. When Building Committees have no time to devote to the study of Architecture, they should, at least, have discretion enough to leave its details to those who have studied them.

‡ Hope alludes to the fact, that this setting up of columns and entablature as a mere screen within an arch occurs in the recesses of the Pantheon. The arrangement there, however, is far less objectionable, than in the case above referred to. The entablature, indeed, crosses the opening between the two points of impost; but there is no open space above it through which the recess is visible. It sustains a species of attic, with panels running entirely around the building.

tunate entablature, it is when it has had its horizontal lines not interrupted only, not merely cut into slips little wider than the diameter of the column below, but even utterly obliterated; has been tortured into a clumsy curve, and made, not to stretch horizontally from column to column, but to circulate, with all its components of architrave, frieze and cornice, around a huge, connecting arch.*

Palace of Diocletian, Spalatro.

The column itself, the leading feature in the classic model, has, in the hands of these Othellos, who "loved not wisely but too well," fared but little better.

The continuous base—the *stylobate*—upon which the long Grecian colonnade solidly and naturally rested, raising the temple from the damps of the earth, and forming the floor of its peristyle; to which the ascent, easy and fitting, was by a magnificent flight of steps, commonly stretching along its entire extent; this solid basement must needs, like the entablature, be cut up into fragments, and these, in the form of squares somewhat wider than the diameter of the column to be supported, must be thrust, under the name of pedestal, beneath the primitive Grecian shaft; cutting off its natural connection with a level and continuous surface, whence, before this intrusion, it had risen simply and gracefully, as its prototype of the forest from the earth: the only result of such intrusion being, to mar the harmony of effect, to obstruct the passage, and to mutilate, past redemption, the simple idea of the original.

Great names, it is true, may be adduced, in favor of the practice of thus stilting the Grecian column upon a narrow and fragmental base. But in our country and in

* This and several other aberrations from purity of style here alluded to, are noticed in Hope's Essay. An American example occurs on the east end of the President's House.

our day, the dicta of great names are not received with blind implicitness.   No architect who knows what is requisite to attain success and eminence in his profession, will fail to make himself familiar with Vitruvius and Palladio; or to study, with care, the imposing structures left behind by the genius of Michael Angelo and of Wren.   But, if he be wise, he will study to examine rather than to believe; taking with him the independent spirit of Paul's injunction, to "prove all things and hold fast that which is good."   It does not follow that he will receive as orthodox Vitruvius' fanciful scale of harmonic proportions; an architectural mystery that has so often exercised, and to so little purpose, the ingenuity of the learned: nor that other analogy, scarcely less fanciful, between the members of Architecture and those of the human frame; even though Michael Angelo sets down this last as a thing so certain, that he declared, an architect must not only have mastered the proportions of the human figure, but, yet more especially, must have studied its anatomy, before he could understand his own profession.*   And thus, too, it may happen, that he will receive, with many grains of allowance, the opinion of the celebrated Vicentine, when he says, of the pedestal, "This part much adds to the beauty and ornament of the work, when it is made with discretion and due proportion of the other parts."†

I have no intention of denying, that there are conditions, for example the restricted space often imposed on street architecture, under which the pedestal may be fairly excused; and others that may even render it strictly appropriate; as in the example given in the annexed cut of an Italian covered well.   But its common and indiscriminate employment, occurring in most of Palladio's designs, and in Roman and Italian Architecture generally, is to be condemned. Its introduction under the columns of the eastern front of our Capitol, materially detracts from the beauty of a noble and impressive elevation.

This offence of the pedestal, however, is but venal compared to others that have been perpetrated, in Roman structures, against the simplicity and independence of the Grecian column.   In

S. Pietro nel Borgo,
Rome.

* His words are:—"E però è cosa certa, che le membra dell'Architettura dipendono dalle membra dell'uomo.   Chi non è stato, o non è, buon maestro di figure, e massime di notomia, non se ne puo intendere."—*Lett.* 17.

† *Palladio,* Book I, c. xix.   In the same chapter he notices the arch of Constantine, at Rome, and gives, without any expression of disapprobation, the proportion of the pedestals there employed, being more than one-third the height of the columns.

the palace of Diocletian, at Spalatro, columns are to be seen supported against the wall on mere brackets, while on these again other columns rest, without even a continued line of separation, to mark an intervening floor. Here, to the vices of inutility and unmeaningness is added another, the semblance of insecurity. It is an essential in a pure style, that every portion of a building should not only *be* solid and safe, but should appear so. When this rule is violated, the effect is uneasy and painful, even when we know there is no just cause for alarm.*

A remarkable example of this falsehood of expression is found in the church of St. Sophia, erected by Justinian at Constantinople. Its architects, Anthemius and Isidorus, in seeking an appearance they ought to have studiously avoided, found a reality and a lesson which ought not to be thrown away upon us.

"By making the pillars destined to support the dome square, and turning the angles towards the centre of the church, so as only to appear the walls or piers that terminated the transepts; and by thus causing the spandrils of the cupola to arise and to spread from the fine line formed by the edges of these angles, they attempted to cause this cupola, of upwards of a hundred feet in diameter, to appear no longer supported even on the four main pillars, but entirely hovering in air, without the least earthly resting-place."†

This specimen of folly and false taste brought down upon its authors a fitting retribution. Though the dome was very lightly constructed, yet in twenty-five years it showed evidences so unequivocal of a speedy downfall, that its architects "thought they could only divert the evil by making amends for the want of more requisite piers within, which would have pleased the eye and mind, by props without, which, by their clumsiness, cause the edifice, externally, to appear a mass of deformity."‡

The warning proved useful in the future. The successors of the St. Sophia architects, says Hope, "condescended to give to the cupolas they raised in air a visible support on earth."

An example in which degenerate taste led to the engrafting on a useful architectural feature of an ornament not incongruous only, but destructive of the very purpose for which the thing ornamented was designed, is instanced by Palladio, in his chapter on abuses, and seems to have been a common practice among his cotemporaries. Speaking of the pedimented and other mouldings introduced above outer doors and windows, not as a mere decoration,

Pendant,
Henry VII.'s Chapel.

---

* Upon this principle alone, if its entire inutility were not reason sufficient, the *pendant* of Gothic Architecture, a feature occurring, for the most part, only in the latest and most degenerate period of that manner, and chiefly in English examples, must be condemned.

† Hope's Essay, p. 114.   ‡ Ibid.

but like the label or dripstone of Gothic Architecture, as a protection from the weather, he says :

"But of all abuses, in my opinion the most intolerable is, the making certain frontons of doors and windows divided in the middle; because these frontons were contrived at first to defend these parts from the wet; so that I know nothing more contrary to natural reason, than to divide and open that part which the ancients did make whole, in order to defend the inhabitants of the house, or those who enter the same, from rain, snow," &c.*

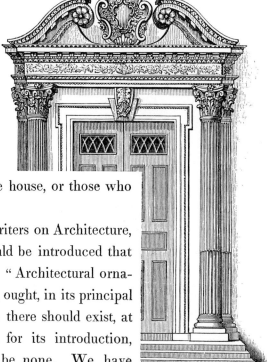

Old Dutch Church, New York.

It is a common rule laid down by writers on Architecture, that no important decorative feature should be introduced that has not the appearance of being useful. "Architectural ornament," says Wilkins, "if not really useful, ought, in its principal parts, to put on the semblance of utility; there should exist, at least in appearance, a sufficient reason for its introduction, although in truth, perhaps, there may be none. We have frequently seen holes or recesses made in walls, for no other purpose but that of containing columns; and it is not uncommon to find little projections formed by sticking a couple of columns with their entablatures, at intervals, along the plain surface of a building. Decoration of this kind is always offensive, because it is at once discovered to originate in an ostentatious desire for splendor; producing infallibly, however, the effect only of tawdry and misplaced finery."†

I advise that no marked or important ornamental features be admitted, unless they not only seem but *are* useful. This seeming, like the superficial forms of politeness, should

---

* *Palladio*, Book I, c. 20. In the same chapter the Vicentine architect notices an example of false style somewhat analogous in character, but showing itself only in minor detail, and which seems to have been prevalent in his time. It was the sustaining of superincumbent weights by sculptured scrolls, instead of columns or pilasters. The scroll must be conceived to represent paper or parchment; and, says he, "since they are feigned to be soft and weak, I know not by what rule they can be put under anything heavy and hard."

An example of pediments broken to introduce busts, where the apex of the pediment should be, may be found in Inigo Jones' Whitehall Palace designs; see "Designs of Inigo Jones," by Kent, 1727; Plate 55.

† Introduction to Vitruvius, p. 10.

CAMPANILE, SMITHSONIAN INSTITUTION,

FROM THE NORTH-EAST.

have something deeper beneath. When, in art or in morals, we once depart from truth, we have neither guide nor stopping-place.*

If to some this analogy seem far-fetched, to them I remark, that any good design will supply a sufficiency of honest occasions, inviting decoration. It is much more necessary to resist those that present themselves than to go in search of others that do not naturally supervene. Better that we refrain from a dozen temptations to legitimate decoration, than yield to one, where ornament is misplaced and superfluous. It is a criticism much to the credit of an architect, that he suffers many tempting opportunities for enrichment to pass by unimproved.

Upon this principle I regard as objectionable the custom, almost universal among architects of the Roman and Palladian schools, of taking from their appropriate station (to wit, the termination of the side walls of the temple *pronaos*) the Grecian *antæ;* repeating these, in somewhat altered form, as pilasters, (resting on bases, surmounted by capitals and marked with entasis,) between window and window, along the entire front of an edifice ; and then, as excuse for their presence, projecting a long slice of entablature, to rest on their summits. As a mere cornice or weather-moulding a projection surmounting the wall of a building requires no such support ;† but if the whole be taken simply as an ornament, devoid of utility, it is too obtrusive and ambitious thus to merit admission. If the projection of the pilaster be too great, as on the flanks of the New York Custom-house, ornament degenerates into deformity ; but, under any ordinary circumstances, I incline to the opinion, that this repetition of pilasters around a building is a feature that cannot be commended.

If it be introduced, as in the Custom-house above referred to, I imagine that it may have been, as a shallow buttress, to strengthen the wall against the thrust of small groined arches, then it is better to adopt at once the flat buttress of the Norman style ; the pilaster-like projection without base, capital or anything else to remind one of the classical pillar ; its surface coinciding with that of the corbel-course above, into which it runs ; or, at other times, terminating so as merely to produce a sort of arch-headed panelling. The effect of this feature in panelling can be judged by inspecting the Campanile tower, standing at the north-east corner of the main building of the Smithsonian Institution; and an example of it, in connection with a Norman

---

* I speak here of *marked* or *important* architectural features. It would be mere over-fastidiousness to insist, in every minor detail of enrichment, on a calculated use or specific purpose. It is, indeed, preferable, in a general way, that, even in these, strict truth of expression should prevail: but where custom or appearance stands in the way, it would be as idle seriously to inveigh, in the case of some trivial ornament, against the aberration, as gravely to impeach the veracity of him, who, on taking leave of a common acquaintance, tells him, he shall be happy to see him again; or, at the close of a formal letter, declares himself to be his correspondent's obedient servant.

† The Farnese palace furnishes an example of the excellent effect with which a bold, massive, crowning cornice can be introduced, without pilasters or engaged columns.

corbel-course, may be seen on the south fronts of the connecting ranges of the same edifice. Its lines are simple and graceful; it is devoid of all pretension, and it can be executed at a trifling cost.

Corbel-course, Smithsonian Institution, Washington.

I have seen it somewhere remarked, justly I think, that the pilaster, as a decoration between windows, is the more objectionable when the windows are devoid of dressing; for in such a case the simpler, and more legitimate because more useful, ornament (the dripstone or weather-moulding to protect the window from wet) is passed by, and the more ambitious and less significant is dragged in.

There is one architectural ornament, dating from a classical era, which cannot, on any principle of utility or just taste, be successfully defended. It is the substitution of Atlantes,* or, still worse, of Caryatides,† for columns. The ancient examples are rare; and the good sense of modern times has caused them to be but rarely imitated. It is but wantonness of fancy, to elaborate a representation of that, which suggests to the imagination an idea painful or revolting.

Temple of Pandrosos.

* Male figures used to support entablatures, &c.; so called by the Greeks, but by the Romans Telamones; and, in modern structures, sometimes Persians. The most remarkable example is the temple of Jupiter Olympius, at Agrigentum, in which the figures were twenty-five feet high.

† Female figures, used as columns for a portico, &c. One of the examples best known, and the only one dating from the classical era of Grecian art, is found in a projection from the flank of the principal Ionic structure, in the triple temple on the Athenian Acropolis.

What taste and ingenuity could effect, Grecian art has effected, in the example in question, (here figured, from Canina.) These failed only because the fault of the conception is inherent and insurmountable. These Caryatides have as much of architectural solidity as could well be given to the female figure. The entablature above might, indeed, have been lighter; yet even if it had been reduced to half its actual depth, the crushing effect upon the figure beneath, which strikes the beholder at the first glance, would not have been avoided.

It is a little remarkable, that, among the various architectural features which the Greeks seem to have borrowed from the Egyptians, this is the only one in which the pupils did not improve on the idea of the original. When Egyptian architects introduced the human figure into their designs, it was in the form of adossed statues, bearing nothing and projecting from the true support of the structure, as may still be seen in the court of the temple of Medinet Habou, or in the adjacent temple of the second Rhamses, (by Danville and Denon spoken of, but erroneously, as the Memnonium;) in the former of which the statues are upwards of twenty-four feet high. This is, unquestionably, far less objectionable than the true caryatid portico; it approaches much more nearly to legitimate sculpture; and its effect, in the example alluded to, is said to be grand and imposing.

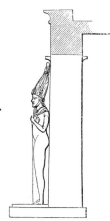

Temple of Medinet Habou.

I have here touched upon some conditions, natural and inherent, that go to make a pure and pleasing style. There are certain conventional laws of taste, of more doubtful authority and less general application, to which, in a subsequent chapter, there will be occasion to allude.

Court in Temple of Medinet Habou, Thebes.

CHAPTER III.

A FEW WORDS CONCERNING THE TWO GREAT DIVISIONS OF MANNER IN ARCHITECTURE.

However various the schools of Architecture in different ages and countries, and how diversified soever the styles into which the mode of each school has been sub-divided, these, in all civilized nations, may be classed under one of two great, distinct-ive manners; to wit, under the head either of POST AND LINTEL ARCHITECTURE, or of ARCH ARCHITECTURE.

Of the former, the two most important examples are the Egyptian and the Grecian. Of the latter, without reckoning a hybrid variety, the Moorish, the Norman or Lombard, and the Gothic, are the principal schools.

The difference between these two manners is radical and inherent. The terms I have selected to designate them point it out.

In all Architecture, public or private, except it be of a purely sepulchral or monumental character, there must be openings, for entrance and exit, for the admission of light and for other purposes. And in all edifices not hypæthral, (that is, open to the sky,) interior spaces of greater or less extent must be covered in, as a shelter from the elements. But upon the mode of covering openings and interiors, more than upon any other one circumstance, the entire manner of Architecture depends.

It is a matter of mere curiosity, and a question solely for the antiquary, whether among the Grecians while their Architecture existed in its purity, or, earlier yet, among the Egyptians or Babylonians, to some individual or other, the principle of the arch may, or may not, have become known; or, in isolated examples, may or may not have been employed in construction. The curious may consult Wilkinson,* Minutoli,† or others. For all practical purposes, that great element of middle-age architecture may be considered as unknown to Egyptian and Grecian builders.‡

---

* " Manners and Customs of the ancient Egyptians."

† " Reise zum Tempel des Jupiter Ammon."

‡ I have seen no sufficient evidence °for the opinion, sometimes expressed, that the arch was employed by Babylonian architects. It is, indeed, known, that bricks were much used in their constructions, and it is true, that, in many cases, the arch has accompanied, or closely followed, the common use of bricks. But bricks were by no means exclusively used in the building of Babylon. Queen Nicrotis' bridge over the Euphrates, if Herodotus may be trusted, had piers of large, hewn stones, connected with iron and

It is evident, that, in the absence of the arch, there was but one mode likely to prevail in practice to cover doors, windows, the spaces of colonnades and other apertures; that is to say, by a horizontal lintel, architrave or bressumer. For the mode occasionally occurring, as in some Saxon examples of door and window heads, formed by placing long stones on end upon the imposts and leaning them against each other at top, so as to form a triangle, was clearly inconvenient and objectionable; and has, therefore, seldom been resorted to, in any style of Architecture.

Deerhurst, Gloucestershire.

When the aperture to be spanned was large, as in covering a spacious interior, imperishable materials were of difficult management. Iron roofs being

lead; and, during the day, pieces of squared wood were laid from pier to pier, which were removed at night, lest the inhabitants on each side should rob one another.—*Herodotus*, i, 178—186.

As to Semiramis' tunnel under the same river, (*Diod. Sic.* lib. ii.) even if it be not somewhat apochryphal, we have evidence that the Babylonians employed other means than the arch to cover in subterranean passages. Mr. Rich, in his interesting "Memoir on Babylon," speaking of one of the mounds found to contain remains of a portion of its ancient buildings, says: "On one side of it a few yards of wall remain standing, the face of which is very clean and perfect, and appears to have been the front of some building. Under the foundations, at the southern end, an opening is made, which discovers a subterranean passage, floored and walled with large bricks, laid in bitumen, *and covered over with pieces of sandstone a yard thick, and several yards long.* The weight above has been so great as to give a considerable degree of obliquity to the side walls of the passage."

Strabo, it is true, asserts, unequivocally enough, that the arch was used in the substructure of the celebrated Hanging Gardens; but he could only have seen Babylon at a period when its public buildings had become heaps of rubbish; and, in this matter, he must have trusted to more ancient authorities, not written from his own observation.

Mr. Rich, in the memoir above referred to, declares: "Notwithstanding the assertion of M. Dutens, there are the strongest grounds for supposing that the Babylonians were entirely unacquainted with the arch, of which I could not find the slightest trace in any part of the ruins, where I purposely made the strictest search."

As to the occasional existence of the arch in very ancient Egyptian structures, some of the best writers concur in asserting it. Wilkinson, who is good authority, says: "I have had frequent occasion to show, that the arch existed of brick in the reign of Amunoph I, (B. C. 1540,) and in stone in the time of Psamaticus, (B. C. 600.)" And he gives an engraving and sections of an arch at Thebes, to which he affixes the date 1500 B. C.—*Wilkinson*, vol. iii, pp. 316, 320, 321.

Belzoni, too, found arches on the Lybian Mountain, and inferred, from what he deemed good authority, that they were older than the Persian conquest.

Nor are we without traces of the arch in ancient Assyrian structures. Layard, in his recently published work, informs us, that, in excavating among the ruins at Nimroud, (that is, on the site of ancient Nineveh,) he penetrated into a wall nearly fifty feet thick, and found, buried in its centre, and without apparent access from without, a "small vaulted chamber built of baked bricks, about ten feet high and the same in width; the arch being constructed on the well-known principle of vaulted roofs." This seems, however, so far as his researches went, to be a solitary example; and, in connection with it, and speaking generally of the field of his observation, he says: "there are no traces of an arch or vault used on a large scale."— *Layard's* "*Nineveh and its Remains*," vol. ii, pp. 41, 260. Authorities vary widely as to the date of the

unknown, beams or joists of wood were brought into use.   Or, when these were not employed, as in the Egyptian examples that have come down to us, a roof of any considerable extent had to be supported, throughout, by perpendicular props.   The flat, terrace roofs of ancient Egypt, without pediment or other projection above the deep-coved cornice that surmounted their entablature, seem to have been composed of flat stones, reaching, either from wall to wall, or from pillar to pillar.   In some cases, as in the Zodiac room in the temple at Denderah, the entire roof was of a single stone.

The Grecian roof, it is true, was a double slant, formed by rafters which leaned against each other, as did the sloping head-stones of the old Saxon window.   But these rafters were framed, at foot, into horizontal tie-beams, so as to overcome their lateral thrust; and the entire frame of the wooden roof exerted upon the side wall or other support that upheld it, a perpendicular pressure only.

The true type, then, of this Architecture, is the horizontal beam or slab, resting upon upright props, the POST AND LINTEL.

The lintel or architrave (*a,*) rests upon the jambs or columns (*b b,*) and the pressure caused by its weight and by all superincumbent weights that may be placed upon it, is a simple pressure upon the sustaining prop, exerted in one direction only, to wit, perpendicularly. If the superincumbent pressure be increased, a single precaution only is demanded, and that is, to increase the number, or enlarge the dimensions, of the sustaining props. If the foundation be good, no other calculation is necessary to assure the safety and solidity of the structure, than an estimate of the weight which the props, be they of wood, stone, or other material, will bear, without being crushed.   No problem of the resolution of forces into downright and lateral pressure requires to be solved.   If the

founding of Nineveh; Ctesias, as quoted by Diodorus Siculus, placing it upwards of two thousand years before Christ, while Herodotus fixes it eight centuries later.   Between Egypt about the period of the eighteenth dynasty (commencing B. C. 1540) and Assyria, there existed a close intercourse.   Taken in connection with this fact, the discovery of the arch in the excavations of Nimroud tends to confirm the opinion of Wilkinson that it existed in ancient Egypt.

Upon the whole, though it seems a thing somewhat strange and anomalous, that an invention of so great utility and universal application in construction as the arch, should have been known and employed at an early period of the world, and should then have been lost, or at least fallen into disuse, for some ten centuries thereafter, it would be hardy to reject the evidence going to prove that such has been the case.

But waiving these inquiries, it suffices for my purpose, that, of all Egyptian and Grecian structures that survive in such preservation as to supply us with examples of these respective styles, the builders either still knew not the arch, or rejected its aid ; adhering, with undeviating strictness, to the post and lintel principle throughout.

pillars or other props are truly set, no side supports are brought into requisition or can be of service.

These conditions stamp upon the Architecture to which they belong, a character of great simplicity, but also of restricted capabilities and of limited expression. Colonnades suggest themselves as its chief ornament. Long, unbroken horizontal lines become a marked and characteristic feature. Except by piling orders upon orders, from which the good taste of Egyptian and Grecian builders studiously refrained, its structures could attain no vast height. The columns of the most spacious and magnificent of the temples of Athens, erected at a cost of more than two millions of dollars, scarcely reached an elevation of sixty feet, though the temple itself was upwards of three hundred and seventy feet in length. Such an Architecture, even in its boldest and grandest specimens, exhibited structures of low and level, and long-stretching outline; massive, quiet, regular; of chaste, severe beauty; and of a uniformity somewhat rigid and monotonous. No projections broke the even surface of its walls, or shot forth, to disturb the continuous line of its colonnades.

This post and lintel manner of Architecture, under forms varying from Stonehenge to the Parthenon, prevailed throughout the earlier ages of the world, and (with exceptions, if exceptions they be, insufficient to invalidate the general rule) probably until some five centuries before the Christian era.* But at last, in a happy moment, it occurred to some philosopher or mechanic, whose name and country† have long since been forgotten, that by arranging small wedge-shaped stones or other materials in a semicircular form, a sort of curved lintel could be obtained, which, though composed of many distinct parts, could be stretched from pier to pier, or from pillar to pillar, with the power of

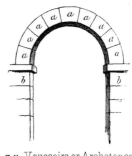

a a, Voussoirs or Archstones.
b b, Points of Impost.

sustaining superincumbent weights far more effectually than the horizontal architrave of a single block.‡

---

* Passing by the mooted question regarding Babylonian and Egyptian arches, it is doubtful whether there be a reliable example of an arched construction of greater antiquity than the *Cloaca Maxima ;* usually referred to the age of the Tarquins.

† Etruria is often named as the probable birthplace of the arch. I have not set down the Etruscan among the principal styles of Arch Architecture, because, though it be undoubtedly one of the oldest among them, it seems to have been, so far as we are now able to judge, a hybrid variety. Of its temples we have no remains. Most of the examples still existing are of sepulchral monuments. Vitruvius characterizes Etruscan buildings as heavy-headed, (" *baricephalæ,*") low and wide. To the Etruscans is ascribed the invention of the dome.

The antiquary may profitably refer to Micali's " *Storia degli Antichi Populi Italiani ;*" also to Inghirami's work, " *Monumenti Etruschi o di Etrusco Nome.*"

‡ There have been, in some stone constructions, what may be regarded as intermediate steps between the lintel and the arch. The triangular heads of some Saxon doors and windows have already been noticed.

Little, in all probability, did the first inventor of the arch imagine, that what may have seemed to him a simple and unimportant discovery was, in its ultimate results, to work an entire revolution, both in forms and principles of construction, in one of the most useful and practical of the productive arts.

The Egyptians very commonly employed a similar form of opening in the entrances to their pyramids. An example here figured, is from the Great Pyramid (of Cheops) at Cairo. In the pyramids of Meroë occurs another form of false arch produced by causing the stones composing the jamb of the opening to project over each other

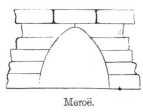

Meroë.

more and more as they approach the top, and then cutting off their edges so as to form a curve. In this way the outline of a pointed arch is obtained; yet the blocks all lie horizontally; there are no wedge-shaped archstones, and, of course, there is no true arch.

Pyramid of Cheops.

The well-known "Gate of Lions," at Mycenæ, (whence, perhaps, issued Agamemnon and his hosts, bound for the conquest of Troy,) exhibits a triangular head, walled up, however, and with a horizontal lintel beneath. The opening, now filled up with rubbish, was probably not less than seventeen feet high. The lions are the most ancient specimen extant of Sculpture in Greece.

Tirynthus.

Gate of Lions, Mycenæ.

There is found, in the walls of Tirynthus, (the ancient capital of Argolis, destroyed before the Trojan war,) a sort of vaulted gallery, but without any true arch; and in the Island of Delos is a construction, of somewhat similar character, here figured from a design of Kinnard; its age not certainly known, but by some supposed to be coeval with the walls of Tirynthus.

Island of Delos.

Yet so it was. Architecture, released, as it were, from its early fetters, acquired powers and capabilities of which Egyptian and Grecian constructors had never dreamed. It had been found a difficult task, even when massive and unwieldy blocks of stone were employed, to cover, with a horizontal lintel of that material, an aperture of more than fifteen or twenty feet. But when the principle of the arch, in its several varieties, became known, the builder discovered, that, by means of small and easily managed blocks of freestone, or even of baked clay, apertures of many times that width could be spanned and covered in. Spacious interiors of imperishable material were thus obtained.

And, as a consequent of the changed mechanical construction, external forms and architectural expression also were revolutionized. A mere pressure of a novel character, the inseparable accompaniment of the new discovery, was the chief agent in this revolution.* The arch, when loaded by superincumbent weight, was found to exert, at its abutment, at either extremity of its span, a pressure of a compound character, partly perpendicular, like that of the horizontal lintel, and partly lateral, having a tendency to thrust outward the pier or wall against which it abutted.† When the weight imposed upon the arch was increased, it became necessary to calculate, not only the perpendicular or crushing pressure which that increased weight exerted in a vertical direction, but also the new element, its lateral thrust. When, in a succession of equal arches, each pier or column upon which these were supported sustained the extremities of two loaded arches springing in opposite directions, the lateral thrust of the one arch was met and neutralized by that, opposed to it, of the other; and per-

* The chief, but not the sole agent. Perhaps the circumstance second only to the arch in its influence upon the revolution, and which is hereinafter noticed at large, was the invention of glass and the introduction of windows as a universal necessity. The window and the column may, in one sense, be said to be antagonistic to each other ; the one admitting light, the other excluding it. The buttress and the window, on the contrary, may (to speak somewhat fancifully) be regarded as natural friends and allies. Attached to the wall, the former does not obstruct or obscure the light that falls on the latter, as do the columns and ceiling of a portico or colonnade ; and, by strengthening the wall along those lines against which alone falls the thrust of the superincumbent vault, the buttress permits openings of any size, for the reception of windows, to be safely made in the spaces intervening between pier and pier.

† The limits and purpose of this treatise render it unnecessary that I should touch upon the theory of the equilibrium of arches ; a subject that has called forth many volumes and much scientific research ; nor that I should notice the results obtained by actual experiments carefully made to determine the points of first failure in the overloaded arch. Enough for my present purpose, that along the flanks of every loaded arch, towards its points of impost or abutment, there is always exerted an outward pressure, greater or less in its degree according to the form of the arch and the amount of weight superimposed.

The subject of the equilibrium of arches is ably treated in the "Mémorial de l'Officier du Génie," vol. xii, (of the original edition.) The experiments above alluded to are by M. Boistard, and are recorded by him in a memoir, entitled "Experiences sur la stabilite des Voûtes," published in the "Recueil de Divers Memoires extraits de la Bibliothèque Imperiale des Ponts et Chaussees." Upon Boistard's experiments is founded the analytic theory of Lagrange, contained in the "Traité de la Construction des Ponts," by Gauthey.

pendicular pressure alone remained.   But at either extremity of such a series of arches

one arch would be found, having its points of abutment, on one side, usually against the external wall of a building, and at these points met by no other neutralizing arch.   It was necessary, therefore, at all such points, to calculate the tendency of the arch to thrust outwards the wall against which one of its extremities rested; and then to overcome that outward thrust by external supports, of greater or less weight and strength, according to the degree of side thrust they were intended to resist.   If that thrust was great, it was sometimes found convenient, in order to give increased solidity and power of resistance to these side supports, to place upon them additional weights.   And these necessities produced

Lady's Chapel, Exeter Cathedral.

the buttress and pinnacle, two of the chief and most characteristic ornaments of that Architecture of which the *Arch* is the fitting type.

In the earliest periods after the discovery of the arch, interiors were covered by the simplest kind of vaulting ; that is to say, by the cylindrical or barrel vault ;* spring-ing from the entire line of two opposite walls, and presenting a uniform concave surface throughout its whole length.† As the lateral thrust of such an arch was exerted equally against the whole line of wall, an increase of thickness throughout was demanded, to resist it. Had no further expedient presented itself, the walls in Arch Architecture would probably have

White Tower, London.

remained plain, massive and comparatively low, as in the earliest Norman examples ; and the structures in the new manner might have retained much of the proportion and general character of the old. But even to Roman architects it occurred, that, instead of suffering the entire line of their barrel vault to abut against a side wall, they might construct, at right angles to it, on either side, a trans-verse vault, or a succession of transverse vaults, cutting into it, so as to result in intersecting ribs and what is called *groined* vaulting. In this way, the pressure, both vertical

Baths of Diocletian.

and lateral, of the entire roof, which had formerly been distributed throughout the whole line of abutment of the barrel vault, became concen-trated at certain points, occurring at intervals along the walls.

When this stage of progress was reached, the foundation was fully laid, whence finally arose the chief features that characterize the Arch Architecture of a later period. For it became evident, that if, at these points of abutment, by means of solid piers, or deep buttresses, the wall was secured, as well

Cathedral of Worms.

against the effects of the outward thrust as of the downward pressure, the essentials to the safety and solidity of the building were already provided.

Working out this theme, with resources hidden from the Greeks ; with a profound knowledge of the mechanical principles of construction, and a thorough acquaintance

---

* The side recesses in the upper room of the United States Patent Office exhibit an example of the barrel vault ; while the centre division of the same room is covered by groined vaulting. One of the hand-somest examples of the barrel vault in this country is the ceiling of the present Library of Congress.

† About the same time that the groined vault was first invented, or adopted as an architectural feature, probably during the reign of Constantine, it appears to have been discovered, that the cylindrical arch would adapt itself to the construction of a spherical dome. This was the germ of that peculiar feature in Roman Architecture, which gave to the *Duomos* of Italy their name, and forms the crowning ornament of many celebrated structures ; of the church of St. Sophia, at Constantinople ; of the Turkish mosque gene-rally, whether found in that city or elsewhere ; and, above all, of St. Peter's and St. Paul's.

with all those mysteries of pressure and counter-pressure, which Sir Christopher Wren himself declared, that he was unable fully to fathom; with an exuberance of fancy, too, which sometimes misled into the whimsical and at last degenerated into the gorgeous; the Free-masons of the Middle Ages gradually elaborated, for Arch Architecture, a system of forms and expressions, the faithful interpreters of its constructive peculiarities, and therefore essentially its own.

The great agent whereby, in this Architecture, the newly-introduced force—the outward pressure exerted by the arch—was overcome, namely, the ponderous, projecting buttress, breaking, at intervals, the uniformity of the outer wall, cutting through all its horizontal lines, and often anchored yet more firmly to the earth by the weight of its lofty, superincumbent pinnacle—that again shooting up, clear through weather-moulding and parapet, and showing, in lines of spirelets, against the sky—this buttress the first and legitimate offspring of the arch, became the leading, external feature of the new Architecture. And then, as a consequent, no more unbroken surfaces, no more level, long-stretching lines, with their continuous masses of broad, horizontal shadow. All was changed. The vertical line, instead of the horizontal, became the ruling principle. To the low and quiet and regular and uniform, succeeded the bold and varied and lofty and aspiring.

And all these changes, thorough and radical and sweeping as they were, owed their first origin to one source; the substitution of the ARCH for the LINTEL.

Stonehenge.

CHAPTER IV.

OF POST AND LINTEL ARCHITECTURE, AND ITS ADAPTATION TO MODERN PURPOSES.

"To the last days of its independence, the Architecture of the Greeks, like a bird still unfledged and incapable of soaring in air, showed what some may call its purity, others its deficiencies."

HOPE'S HISTORICAL ESSAY.

OF the two chief varieties of this Architecture, it has never been seriously contended that the Egyptian, with its colossal porticos and its gigantic masses and its endless sculpture, is suitable for general imitation, or adapted to modern purposes, among us. Some of its forms, indeed, possess elegance, and produce architectural effects legitimate and striking of their kind; and therefore well worthy of study.

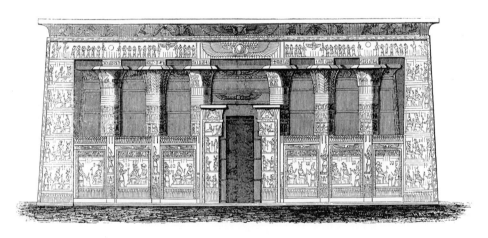

Temple of Edfou.*

The sloping outline of its ponderous walls shows well in contrast with its rigid columns; but that form of wall is troublesome and expensive in construction, and weathers badly; the lower portion of the wall being usually projected beyond the drip of its cornice. For monumental purposes, as the architecture of cemeteries, the

* This temple, here figured from Gailhabaud's "Ancient and Modern Architecture," is one of the most interesting and complete in the whole valley of the Nile. It stands on the left bank of that river, about fifty-five miles above Thebes. It is four hundred and fifty-four feet long by two hundred and fourteen wide.

Egyptian is suitable enough.   It has been proposed for railroad entrances and stations; and a Philadelphian architect* has employed it, with good features, in prison construction.   But beyond these occasional adaptations, it is clearly unwieldy and impracticable; and may, therefore, in the present connection, be dismissed without further comment.†

The Grecian model remains; that Architecture the purest and most finished of its kind; of which some of the examples, surviving twenty centuries of duration, are pronounced by many to have been unsurpassed—unequalled even—throughout all that long lapse of years.

When we talk of imitating, or adopting, in modern structures, the Grecian style of Architecture, we speak indefinitely and inaccurately.   Of the domestic constructions of the Greeks, as of the Romans in the better days of their Republic, we know little, except that they had no pretensions, in their exterior, to decorative or architectural character.   Custom, or a religious sentiment, interdicted, in the dwelling of the pri-

* Haviland, architect of "The Tombs," New York.

† I have not here alluded to an ancient and primitive phase of post and lintel architecture, still existing in certain Celtic remains, because these are valueless to the architect, however interesting to the antiquary. The chief among them are what are sometimes termed *fairy grottoes* or *fairy rocks*; of which the example the most remarkable, perhaps, for the size of its blocks and for its excellent preservation, is the " Roche

Roche aux Fées, near Saumur, France.

aux Fées," near Saumur, on the road to Bagneux.   This Cyclopean monument is about fifty-eight feet long by fifteen feet wide.   The roof, after the fashion of Egyptian Architecture, is flat and covered by huge blocks of stone, four only in number; the largest being nearly twenty-three feet square.   This enormous table is cracked from end to end, and is supported by an upright stone, standing isolated in the centre.

vate citizen, the forms and adornments employed in edifices of a sacred character. We read that Julius Cæsar himself deemed it necessary to procure permission, by a special decree of the Senate, before he ventured to adorn the front of his house with a *fastigium* or pediment.*

And, even as regards public buildings, in the early days of pure Grecian Architecture, these were, with exceptions not worth noticing, of one description only; temples to the gods.

To speak with accuracy, then, we ought to talk of adapting to modern purposes the architecture of a Grecian temple.

But, on the face of it, the chance of managing such adaptation with advantage and propriety, does not seem very promising. The purposes for which, among the Greeks, a temple was employed; the rigidly regular form to which it was usually restricted; the climate in which it was erected; the ignorance, in those days, of one of the most important principles of construction, as well as of the modern mode of admitting light while excluding wind and rain; all conspire to diminish the probabilities, that the temple model of two thousand years ago can be reproduced, advantageously, to-day, among us.

Nothing can be more simple or inartificial, than the common plan of the Grecian temple. Four plain walls enclosed a rectangular space, the *cella* or *naos*, generally about twice as long as wide, and usually surrounded by a colonnade, or *peristyle*, supported on a single row of columns, occasionally on a double row. Sometimes, especially in temples to the superior gods, the interior of the cella was left, in whole or in part, open to the sky; so that the edifice (if it be in strictness entitled to the name) was, in fact, little more than a quadrangular colonnade. And even without reference to such a peculiarity, the cella, in the more sumptuous examples, became, as

Hope has expressed it, "a small nut or kernel, contained in a prodigious envelope;" as from the annexed ground-plan, showing the proportions of the cella in the Athenian Temple of Jupiter Olympius, to its magnificent peristyle, may readily be gathered.

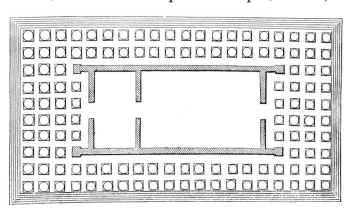

Temple of Jupiter Olympius, Athens.

When the temple was covered in, it was with a wooden roof, tiled or flagged; of low pitch, and

* *Cic. Phil.* ii, 43.

5

terminating, at either extremity of the rectangle, in a triangular pediment. In the centre of one or both of the short sides of the rectangle, there was a spacious door; but, in what are regarded as the purest examples of the style, there were no windows; and it has usually been held, that, to give full effect to a Grecian colonnade, there is required, behind it, in contrast with its columns, an unbroken uniformity of wall.

The columns of a Grecian temple were commonly placed so close to each other, that the open space between them was less than a diameter and a half of the column. And the usual distance from the column to the wall of the cella, was but little greater. Even with this intercolumniation, the horizontal blocks or lintels composing the architrave (the *epistylia*) became ponderous and of difficult management; being, in the larger temples, from twelve to twenty feet in length. In what Vitruvius has called the *arœostyle* order of temple, the columns are set more sparsely, their centres being four, or even five, diameters apart; but this intercolumniation was never adopted by the Greeks; and Vitruvius reminds us, that, whenever it is employed, stone or marble cannot be used for the architrave, but "beams of durable timber must be employed for the purpose."

The law, then, which prescribed his *eustyle* intercolumniation* is of easy interpretation. It was the stern law of necessity; and it remained in force until the discovery and application of the arch.†

The Grecian temple was, in all cases, but one story in height; and it need hardly be added, that, even when covered in from the elements, it had no chimneys, or other means of artificial warmth.

Its purpose was, to do honor to the god, or goddess, whose name it bore, and to serve as an imposing locality for the exhibition of religious sacrifices and other ceremonial rites. Sometimes, also, it was employed as a treasury.

---

* That is, with a distance of two diameters and a quarter, from centre to centre. This Vitruvius sets down as the most elegant. It is the usual proportion in Doric colonnades. The columns of the Parthenon were somewhat less than six feet in diameter. This gives the length of blocks in its architrave, between thirteen and fourteen feet.

† The usual intercolumniation in the Corinthian order, is about three diameters. In the Girard College, in consequence, as I imagine, of the dimensions of the building being prescribed in the will of the founder, the architect has stretched his intercolumniation to upwards of three diameters and a half, giving to his epistylia a length of twenty-one feet five inches. He was afraid to trust these on the principles of Grecian construction. He informs us, in his Final Report, that he "deemed it prudent to relieve these architraves of all superincumbent weight, by resolving it directly on the columns." "This," he proceeds to state, "is accomplished by placing a block of granite of two feet by two feet ten inches, and six feet four inches in height, on the top of each column, extending through the architraves. From the top of these blocks, a brick arch is turned over each intercolumniation behind the frieze, to receive the weight of the cornice. The frieze is also constructed on the principles of an arch, and is kept clear of the architrave."

Here is an example of that falsehood of expression, and masking of constructive relation, to which, in a subsequent chapter on Hybrid Architecture, I shall have occasion specially to allude.

Now, it is difficult to imagine anything in the shape of a public edifice further removed, in purpose and adaptation, from modern wants in a climate like ours, than this rectangular cell, with its magnificent accessories. If, indeed, it were required to design, as a summer promenade, a quadrangular colonnade of great richness and admirable proportions, without reference to cost, one might find, in the temple of Attica or Ionia, a model equally elegant and suitable. But when there is question of a public building, to be used for such purposes as public buildings, in our day, are commonly put to, and at such cost as modern congregations or other public bodies are usually willing to incur, the case is wholly different.

We know the use of glass, though the Greeks did not; we have chimneys, though the Greeks had none; we can span wide apertures with the arch, though the Greeks were ignorant of the invention; and we have a climate subject to snow-storms and to tempests, very different from the mild and equable climate of Greece.

But this is not all. Our domestic habits, our public customs, our religious exercises, are all wholly different from those of the Greeks. We enter a church for the purpose of hearing a discourse or other religious exercise, not to assist at a sacrifice, or as mere spectators of some other ceremony. And, therefore, in our religious edifices, no less than in halls erected for purposes of legislation, or of public justice, or literature, we desire to be comfortably seated, in a building duly warmed, according to the season; effectually lighted, by day as well as night; and of such size and form as to be easily within compass of the human voice. And these conveniences, even when combined under the forms of an architecture of pleasing and creditable exterior, we usually expect to obtain at a moderate cost.

How are we to obtain these objects, and yet preserve the characteristic beauties that have so long delighted the world in the classical model?

In the first place are we to retain the peristyle—the colonnade surrounding the Grecian cella? If we do not, then we discard, at once, what all admirers of classic Architecture concur in regarding as its distinguishing and most characteristic feature.* We may, indeed, cut it down to a portico, at one or at both ends of the cell, and we have classical precedents enough for so doing. But if, as is too frequently the case, we rest satisfied with this simple adjunct, deeming our task completed when we have examined the proportions of its pediment, and the details of its columns and entablature, and leaving the rest of the building carelessly to its fate, then we have a structure

---

* " L'économie ou d'autres causes ont porté quelquefois les Peuples qui se sont distingués dans l'Architecture, à faire des portiques ; il n'en est pas moins prouvé par les faits, qu'ils ont toujours préféré les peristyles à ces portiques ; et que ce sont de toutes les décorations celles qui nous font éprouver les sensations les plus agréables."—*Essai sur la Théorie de l'Architecture ; by Le Roi, Historiographer of the Royal Academy of Architecture. Paris, fo., 1770.*

without unity or consistency of decoration, elaborately ornamented in one part, and neglected, without apparent cause, in another: we are but reminded of a magnificence to which the architect evidently aspired, though he could not succeed in attaining it. This defect is the greater where the decorative feature, thus singly appended, is one of much pretension, of great expense, and of no obvious necessity. It is, at all times, a dangerous thing to meddle with a style of ambitious decoration. Unless our purse be of the deepest and our judgment of the best, we are much more likely to suggest what is omitted than to satisfy with what is done.

But the longing after economical splendor has led much further than the mere curtailment of the Grecian peristyle. The materials and workmanship of the best examples of the ancient temple were of the most costly description. The Parthenon, with fluted columns nearly six feet in diameter at the base, was wrought throughout in the most durable marble and with the exquisite finish of a cameo; containing a range of eleven hundred feet of sculpture, including upwards of six hundred figures, of which a portion were colossal. To the omission of the sculpture, an incidental enrichment, there can, evidently, be no objection; but when the Doric columns and splendid entablature of that noble pile are repeated in brick and disguised with plaster, which every trifling accident breaks off, discovering the cheat beneath, the result, like that of tawdry finery, is untruthful and meretricious. It is the mere glitter of riches, without the reality. And this effect is felt the more strongly, because the predicament is one of free choice. There is no law requiring us to attach to one end of a public building a classical portico, or to encompass it with a Grecian colonnade, when the means at our disposal are insufficient to execute either, in a decent or reputable manner. There is always the alternative, and just taste enjoins it, to adopt a plainer and cheaper style, such as our funds will enable us to carry out truly and faithfully, without pretence or makeshift. And if we will not do this, we have little right to complain if we feel the smart of those shafts of criticism, to which, at the instigation of overvaulting ambition, we had wilfully and needlessly exposed ourselves. It is a rule of good taste to which, in all cases where ornament is thus volunteered, there is no exception, that what cannot be done well should not be attempted at all.

But let us take a case, like that of the Girard College of Philadelphia, in which the funds are ample, and those charged with the erection decide to carry out the Grecian peristyle honestly and appropriately, in marble* that may rival that drawn

* Chiefly from quarries in Montgomery and Chester Counties, Pennsylvania; partly from Egremont, Massachusetts.

Marble of excellent quality is found in many parts of the United States. A portion of that quarried in the vicinity of Clarksville, Maryland, a village some thirteen miles from Baltimore, on the line of the Susquehanna Railroad, is fine-grained and of a beautifully uniform color, approaching the character of statuary marble.

from the quarries of Pentelicus, and in a style of workmanship worthy of such material; the inquiry remains, whether the genuine temple model, which, as a mere work of art, will always command admiration, has been wisely adopted; and whether, in any modern structure, its advantages compensate for its cost.

We are not likely to carry our love for the pure Grecian so far, as to discard glass, because it was unknown to the classical builder, and to light modern interiors with lamps or torches. We must condescend, then, to the commonplace convenience of windows behind our colonnade; even though it go sadly against the grain, with the architect, to break up the walls of his cella and mar the harmony of his peristyle, with any such prosaic interpolation. Nor will a single row of these satisfy the urgency of modern wants. We must needs have our modern buildings two or more stories high; as in the case, for example, of the Treasury Building at Washington, of which the Ionic columns cut across three tiers of windows, with a very unclassical effect.

Here is the first point of difficulty. The colonnade is ill adapted to any modern system of fenestration. Yet it is not alone that glass windows harmonize but indifferently with marble columns; these latter, especially in a climate subject to frequent clouds and tempests, destroy, in a measure, the object of the former. They materially obstruct the light; as the clerks in the Treasury Department, especially those in the upper range of rooms, of which the windows look out immediately beneath the massive entablature, know to their cost.

The columns of a regularly proportioned Doric peristyle cover up about *two-fifths* of the entire front space, the openings making up the remaining three-fifths. In Ionic and Corinthian colonnades, the proportion of the openings is somewhat greater; but even in the latter, the lighter and more slender of the two, the columns usually fill one-third of the front space. It will be readily perceived, that such obstructions must very materially darken the light in all the rooms behind them.

And this must be considered a very serious objection to the peristyle of the Greeks, in modern constructions; since there are few buildings among us, whether public or private, in which it is not desirable, that each room should be sufficiently lighted to enable its inmates to read and write with facility, in every part of it, even in the cloudiest weather. We cannot reasonably forego such advantages, for the purpose of perpetuating the Architecture of a former age. As rationally might we still transact most of our business in the open forum, as the Romans, escaping from their darkened rooms, were wont to do.*

The expense at which the light is thus classically obstructed, remains to be considered.

* Our own ancestors, in some of the old English country towns, used to transact their legal business in buildings not exactly hypæthral, but consisting of little more than a mere naked frame, with a roof. In those days the phrase, " coming into open court," was often a very literal one. These primitive halls were

The cost of each column in the peristyle of the Girard College is, according to the statement of the architect, twelve thousand nine hundred and ninety-four dollars. There are thirty-four columns. There has been expended, therefore, for the columns alone, the sum of *four hundred and forty-one thousand seven hundred and seventy-six dollars*. If it be said, that a portion of this vast cost results from the selection of the richest and most ornate of the Grecian orders, the reply is that furnished by the architect. The height of the building, which was prescribed by the will, determined also the height of the colonnade. And if either of the other orders had been selected, inasmuch as the height of the column determines its diameter, and as either order requires a shaft of more massive proportion than the Corinthian, the cost would have been even greater than that actually incurred. Mr. Walter says:

" Had the Ionic order been adopted, the marble for a single column would have cost, at the rate of that paid for the present order, about fourteen thousand five hundred dollars; or fifteen hundred dollars more than the whole cost of the present column, including workmanship. The Doric order would have been still more expensive, if, indeed, the material could have been procured at any price, as it would have required columns of nine and a half feet in diameter." *

It is evident, then, that in a colonnade either Doric or Ionic around the same building, the columns alone, if of marble, would have cost upwards of half a million of dollars.

In order to obtain the cost of the Girard College peristyle, we must add to the

open not only to justice but to the wind and weather also. Some curious examples still remain, as in the town of Huntingdon; though the spirit of modern improvement is fast sweeping them away.

Glass was not an article of common use in England, even three centuries ago. Though as early as the year 674 artists were brought to England from abroad to glaze the church windows at Weremouth in Durham, yet even as late as the year 1567 glass was still confined to large dwellings, and was by no means universal in them. An entry made in that year in the minutes of a survey of Alnwick Castle, the residence of the Dukes of Northumberland, informs us, that the glass casements were taken down, during the absence of the family, to preserve them from accident.

Open Court-House, Huntingdon.

* Final Report of the architect, Thomas U. Walter, to whose kindness I am indebted for the various items connected with the cost of this edifice.

cost of the columns above given, that of the entablature and of the stylobate, with its steps, eleven in number, and extending entirely around the building; also that proportion of the roof by which the colonnade is covered. These items amount to about two hundred and forty-five thousand six hundred and thirteen dollars; and thus we have the entire cost of the colonnade, reaching the sum of six hundred and eighty-seven thousand three hundred and eighty-nine dollars.

As to the extent of the covered promenade obtained at so enormous a cost, the clear space in the colonnade of the Parthenon between the columns and the side walls of the cella was but about nine feet. The columns outside of this narrow walk being forty-two feet in height, it is evident that it was very imperfectly sheltered from drifting rain or snow.

In the Girard College the covered space is somewhat wider in proportion; being about fourteen feet clear of the columns; but, as the columns themselves are fifty-five feet high, to the ceiling of the peristyle, rain driven by the wind at a trifling slant would drift across the peristyle floor, even to the walls of the cella.

It should be remembered, also, that in the Girard College, as in the temple model generally, there are but two entrances from without; one in the centre of each of the ends of the cella. A porch at each of these would afford effectual protection; and no colonnade, or covered walk, is required, to afford sheltered communication between numerous doors of exit. As a dry and somewhat protected promenade, the peristyle in question is, without doubt, of a certain utility.

The erection of this sumptuous colonnade around an institution building destined to receive, for education, penniless orphans, has been justified on the ground, that it is "of use in forming the mind, and moulding the manners, of the children of poverty."* That the habitual presence of the beautiful in art exerts a humanizing and cultivating influence on the young mind is a truth, of which the importance is often overlooked. Yet, if I may be allowed, without incurring the imputation of vandalism, to throw into a plain, matter-of-fact, business form, a question in æsthetics, I invite attention to the following estimate. The Girard College might have been finished externally, in a handsome and appropriate manner, and with great advantage to the solidity of the structure, with Gothic buttresses and pinnacles, say seven on each side and four on each end. These, with a handsome carriage porch at either entrance, would not have cost, to estimate liberally, more than from ninety to a hundred thousand dollars. Deduct this sum from the cost of the colonnade, and there remains, say five hundred and ninety thousand dollars. As money may be considered worth six per cent., the above expenditure to obtain a Grecian instead of a Gothic exterior,

* "Address on placing the Crowning Stone of the Girard College," by Joseph R. Chandler.

may be regarded as an outgoing of upwards of *thirty-five thousand dollars a year*, *for ever ;* expended to produce on the minds of three hundred young boys, whatever balance of civilizing influence the daily sight of a Grecian peristyle may be supposed to exert on these youths, over and above that which the habitual contemplation of a graceful Gothic edifice may be calculated to produce. Whether this difference be worth its cost is a question, in regard to which I confess my astonishment, that, among intelligent men, there should be two opinions.*

We have seen that the Grecian manner, followed out in its purity, presents serious obstacles to any system of fenestration by which a modern building may be effectually lighted. It lends itself, with equal reluctance, to any efficient plan of warming and ventilation.

In the language of the classical architect, a chimney is a sordid object. He regrets its necessity, and tasks his ingenuity to mask and conceal its existence, as a blemish in his plan.

This is false taste. The Greeks showed no chimneys in their temples, because they had none; because, in their sunny climate, they required none. In such a climate, a building without apparent means of artificial warmth, is felt to be suitable and appropriate. But in one of the snow-storms of our climate, the effect is bleak and chilly and comfortless. We know that a building ought to have fires in winter; and the evidence of their existence is a cheerful and a pleasant thing. In other manners, the Gothic, for example, the evidence of warmth within, the chimney, not only ceases to be a blemish, but becomes

Distant Effect of Gothic Chimneys,
St. Osyth's Priory

---

* The cost in question amounts to *one hundred and sixteen dollars annually, for each orphan ;* an income sufficient, if administered with strict economy, to support and educate them out and out.

If any one be still inclined to question the justice of the opinion expressed above, I beg him to reflect, what a magnificent collection of paintings, of sculpture, of objects of art and of natural history, of books—in a word, of all civilizing and cultivating influences—the judicious expenditure of thirty-five thousand dollars a year might gradually bring together.

It would not require a single year's expenditure to procure a series of models in cork, that would explain and illustrate, better than years of verbal explanation, the characteristic forms and peculiar adaptations of every school of Architecture, ancient and modern.

ornamental. And if its upright lines and projecting stacks of flues, seem out of place and show awkwardly from behind the *antefixæ* of the temple eaves, or the sloping line of its pediment, that is but an additional reminder, that we ought to be cautious in implicitly transferring to one climate the Architecture of another.

Exton, Rutland.

Tonbridge School, Kent.

It sometimes happens, that chimneys, or ventilating flues, are required of so great a height, that, standing alone, they must appear, in any style, a lank and toppling and awkward object. In such a case, the classical architect is wholly without resource. He cannot, by any device, mask a lofty shaft, shooting up above his flat, temple roof; since towers, spires, pinnacles, and all similar aspiring barbarisms are to him interdicted forms. Not so, in a Norman or Gothic design. The case occurred, in planning a portion of the Smithsonian building. In its east wing, destined for a Laboratory and Chemical Lecture-room, several flues, some sixty feet high, were considered necessary to produce draft for wind furnaces, intended for crucible and other smelting operations, where high heats were required. These were obtained within a bell-tower, of the old Norman form; serving also, like those from which in the olden time the curfew once sounded, the purpose which its name implies; and surmounting, picturesquely and appropriately, the centre of the eastern elevation.

Smithsonian Institution.

As the Grecian temple was a single story only in height, staircases were unnecessary.* These can, indeed, under ordinary circumstances, be obtained by encroaching on one or both ends of the cella, as in the Girard College. Or, in modernized

---

* The classical architect usually regards this feature as embarrassing. Palladio, speaking of staircases, says, it is difficult to find a place convenient for them, that will not, at the same time, prejudice the rest of the building.

6

Grecian, they may cut into the centre of the main front. But there are cases in which such an arrangement is inconsistent with the plan and purpose of a public building. It is sometimes required, that an upper story shall be occupied by one large room, unbroken, in the centre, by vestibule or stairway, and extending, at each end, to the outer walls, so as to permit end windows. Such a case presented itself in two different portions of the Smithsonian edifice. It was judged expedient, that the upper story of the main building should be occupied, in its entire length, by a single apartment, to serve the purposes of a museum. This was effected by running up the staircases within central towers, projecting in front and in rear; these towers harmonizing well with the style adopted;* affording small apartments, which were indispensable; and lending themselves to the architectural effect of the structure, both by giving it elevation, which, in its somewhat low and flat site overlooked by Capitol Hill, it wanted, and much increasing its breadth, as seen from the east or west; this latter item being important, inasmuch as the internal adaptations of the main building had given to it a width of but fifty to a length of two hundred feet, and that length again had been more than doubled by the addition of the wings and connecting ranges.

Another case in point occurred in planning the east wing. The entire rectangle of that wing was laid out as a Chemical Lecture-room, with a gallery on three sides, and, on the fourth side, a Laboratory adjoining the Lecture-room and opening into it. It was decided, that the seats in the main body of the Lecture-room should be placed on an inclined surface, rising to the gallery floor and connecting with it; and that the usual entrance for the audience should be, not below, where delicate and fragile apparatus was exposed, but by a staircase to the gallery floor, whence the audience should descend, on either side of the inclined plane, to its seats. To carry into effect this arrangement, a stairway outside the Lecture-room was required. It was obtained within a porch projecting from the eastern front; and as, in a porch of suitable proportions, the requisite height could not be gained without making the stairs too steep, a small outer porch was added, with a few steps therein.

Thus the peculiarities of internal adaptation in this wing stamped upon its eastern elevation the exterior it now presents; the general effect being, I think, pleasing and harmonious.†

Again, it was thought proper, in addition to the main entrance from the south, to provide a private stairway, conducting to the Regents' and Secretary's rooms, in the upper stories of the central southern tower. A small octagonal tower supplied this

---

* The central towers of the principal front are given in the frontispiece; and a view of the main tower on the south front faces the next page.

† See general view of the Institution building, south front, given in Chapter IX.

CENTRAL SOUTHERN TOWER, SMITHSONIAN INSTITUTION;

FROM THE SOUTH-WEST.

convenience; and this fortuitous accessory will be generally admitted to have improved, instead of marring, the effect of this portion of the edifice.

But now let us suppose, that, as in the case of the Girard College, the Grecian temple had furnished the model for the Institution building, and it is evident, that these various internal arrangements must have been abandoned, a sacrifice to external uniformity. For what architect would adventure a staircase constructed outside the cella, and breaking into his Grecian peristyle? Even in an edifice which follows, with far less strictness, the temple model, namely, the United States Patent Office, the architect, to obtain an unbroken exhibition-hall extending throughout the second floor of his building, had to throw out, in the centre of its northern front, a semicircular projection; a feature for which, in ancient classical Architecture, we shall seek a precedent in vain.

So serious are the obstacles presented by the rigid and uncomplying forms of the classical school, that internal convenience is often sacrificed upon the altar of antique taste. The man is not to be measured for the garment, but is to be fitted into it. The foot is not to determine the size and form of the shoe; but the shoe, as of the Chinese lady, is prescribed; and the foot must conform to its shape and dimensions.

Lyell, the geologist, in his " Travels in North America," gives some striking examples of the extent to which this sacrifice of internal adaptation to obtain a showy exterior, has sometimes been carried. Speaking of the London University, erected at a cost of half a million dollars, of which one-third was spent on the portico and dome, he says: " When the professor of Chemistry inquired for the chimney of his laboratory, he was informed, that there was none; and, to remove the defect, a flue was run up, which encroached on a handsome staircase, and destroyed the symmetry of the architect's design. Still greater was the dismay of the anatomical professor, on learning, that his lecture-room was to conform to the model of an ancient theatre, designed for the recitation of Greek plays. Sir Charles Bell remarked, that an anatomical theatre, to be perfect, should approach as nearly as possible, to the shape of a well, that every student might look down and see distinctly the subject under demonstration. At a considerable cost the room was altered, so as to serve the ends for which it was wanted."

In the case of a rival Institution, to which the public contributed a liberal endowment, there seems to have been as little judgment exercised. Lyell informs us, that "when the professor of Chemistry at King's College asked for his laboratory, he was told it had been entirely forgotten in the plan, but that he might take the kitchen on the floor below, and, by ingenious machinery, carry up his apparatus, through a trap-door, into an upper story, where his lecture-room was placed."*

* *Lyell's Travels*, vol. i., p. 113.

These glaring errors are the more remarkable, since, in the arrangement and erection of two of the leading scientific institutions of Great Britain, we may suppose the best professional talent of that island to have been employed.

It is strange, that, at this day, it should be necessary to repeat, that, in planning any edifice, public or private, we ought to begin *from within ;* that we should first suffer the specific wants and conveniences demanded, to block out its forms, to determine its interior proportions and decide the connection of its parts ; and then adjust and elaborate its architecture as its appropriate garb ; into the skilful fashioning of which there enter, in truth, grace and fair proportions, but yet in such guise, that the garment shall adapt itself to the individual form it is destined to clothe ; fitting well, and displaying the peculiarities of that form to the best advantage.

But when we reflect within what narrow limits, in the antique school, latitude is given to depart from the ordained scale of classical proportions ; and how few data need be given to stamp upon a regular Grecian edifice, with only such slight variations as are permitted within these limits, its exact form and size and character,* it cannot surprise us, that an orthodox Vitruvian should abandon, in despair, the hopeless task of interpreting, in an architectural language two thousand years old, interior purposes, dispositions, adaptations, which have all had birth since that language reached its perfection ; or of effecting a compromise between the infinite variety of forms springing from those manifold modern purposes, and the few and uniform and imperative phases of exterior among which alone he is permitted to make selection.

It should not be subject of regret, but rather of gratulation, that a striving after excellence in Architecture has caused copies of the classical model, in its chief varieties, to arise among us. These are profitable and cultivating subjects of study ; as, indeed, are all structures stamped with a truly national manner. It would be an advantage to us, if a taste which might be set down as whimsical were to furnish us occasional examples of other national styles, even if less meritorious than the Grecian ; as the Egyptian, the Chinese, the Saracenic. It is only after extensive comparison that just judgments are formed. And as in almost all systems of polity that have won so far on the hearts and judgments of mankind as to become national, so is it in the department of art. We may draw valuable lessons, we may gather useful hints, from much of the past ; and this not the less, that it is seldom we can adopt with implicitness, or commend without reservation.

---

* "If the dimensions of a single column, and the proportion the entablature shall bear to it were given to two individuals acquainted with the style, with directions to compose, in the Doric order, a hexastyle peripteral temple (that is, with six columns in front and a colonnade around the cell) or one of any other description, they would produce designs exactly similar, in size, arrangement, features and general proportions ; differing only, if it all, in the relative proportions of minor parts, and slightly, perhaps, in the contour of some of the mouldings."—*Art. Architecture, Encyclopedia Britannica,* p. 434.

It is not alone as regards exteriors that the temple Architecture of Greece is indocile and uncomplying. Its interiors, imperfectly lighted, were, comparatively, an unimportant feature; sometimes, as in hypæthral temples, dispensed with altogether. Its magnificence, with all its most graceful, distinguishing features, was external. The clustered pillar of a Gothic or Norman cathedral, with its shafts attached for the purpose of vaulting, essentially belongs to an interior. Not so the classical column. The upper member of its entablature, the projecting cornice, is a weather-moulding, which fulfills its purpose when it surmounts an outer wall or a peristyle; but is out of place in any situa-

tion, whence the elements are already excluded. If such a member, regardless of the intention which originally gave it form and place, is to be taken within doors and set up there, merely because we have been accustomed to see and admire it, in exteriors, surmounting the frieze and architrave, it is difficult to say why the roof should be left outside.

Baptistery of Pisa, Italy.

To the column of the Grecian peristyle, as an interior feature, when it is surmounted by its architrave alone, as an impost for a gallery, or even for an arch, there is, indeed, not the same objection. Palladio has thus used it; as also have other architects, in various Roman edifices, but more especially in Lombard or Romanesque interiors, (the Baptistery of Pisa, for example) happily enough. Yet, even in such a connection, the Grecian column suggests no peculiar fitness, no special or calculated adaptation, when employed as an interior feature; and in cases where the ceiling is vaulted, it is manifestly out of place

But this would lead me to speak of that transition style of Architecture, commonly called Roman, and, as it approached the confines of the Gothic, Romanesque, in which an endeavor was made to clothe a new principle in an old dress ; and to which, as it brought together discordant elements, producing, in their forced union, nothing permanent or distinctive, I think the epithet of *hybrid* may properly be applied.

In this hasty review of the merits and adaptations of the classical school, I have treated of these, not with reference to their intrinsic excellence, but in connection with their availability in a modern world. I have but sought to show, that the Grecian can never truly become our Architecture ; seeing that a true Architecture should serve, not dictate ; should minister to the wants of man, not demand, that these wants should be squared and formalized and schooled down, till they conform to the measure of its arbitrary preconceptions.

That the Grecian model has, in the progress of civilization, become thus arbitrary and exacting, is no disparagement to its original merit. No mind alive to a perception of the beautiful in art, but must regard the temple of Greece as a pure and admirable creation. It must have been beautiful indeed, in the first freshness of its exquisite workmanship. It is beautiful still, in ruins.

Temple of Segesta.

CHAPTER V.

OF HYBRID ARCHITECTURE.

"The Romans, had they been possessed of a delicate appreciation of the beauties of art, had they been gifted with inventive or imaginative fancies, would, for their arch, have devised some new species of ornamental addition, appearing to belong to its nature and composition."

HOPE'S HISTORICAL ESSAY.

THE post and lintel manner of Architecture had its faithful and graceful interpreters among the Greeks. Tied down to the only mode then known of spanning openings and covering interiors, and thus compelled, whenever they excluded wood from an edifice, to approach its props, or supporting posts, closely to each other, they made the most of the narrow limits to which they were confined. As a support at once appropriate and beautiful, to sustain perpendicular pressure—the only one exerted by their lintel—they elaborated the classical column, that triumph of Grecian art; and so justly did they proportion, and so happily design, and so tastefully, even to its minute details, did they work out this, the favorite and dominant feature of their Architecture, that it retained favor and station for centuries after radical changes had supervened, which, followed out to their legitimate results, materially affected its usefulness and suitability.

The arch, with its compound pressure, side-thrusting as well as downright, was invented and applied. But as men ever reluctantly abolish the forms to which they have been accustomed, architects were slow to perceive, what changes were rendered necessary or appropriate by this invention. They borrowed for it the Grecian costume; and continued thus to clothe it with garments not belonging to it, for so long a period of time, that when, at last, the Free-masons of Northern Europe invested it in its own peculiar and characteristic garb, the sticklers for classical precedent saw in the change nothing but whim and heresy, and stigmatized some of the noblest efforts of architectural genius as barbarous and *Gothic*.*

I have already set forth, as lying at the basis of all true Architecture, the principle,

---

* Palladio calls the Gothic " that old way of building which is without any proportion or grace at all." *Book II, Chap.* 3.

A native of Vicenza, in Northern Italy, Palladio flourished in the sixteenth century, dying in 1580.

that external form should be the faithful interpreter of internal purpose. It follows, that when there is introduced into practical construction any element of change, of a nature so radical, as intrinsically to affect an architectural system; to alter the relative proportions, and to vary the forms, that make up its anatomical condition; that new element should affect also its extrinsic or superficial character. In such a case we are not only justified in modifying or discarding conventional laws of taste, framed to suit other circumstances, but reason and propriety enjoin it upon us so to do.

Now such an element as this, so radical in its influence on the entire framework of Architecture, so thorough in the changes, both of form and proportion, to which it led, was the arch, with its far-reaching powers of support, and that lateral thrust, or oblique pressure, which inseparably accompanies it.

By its intervention all necessity for that proximity of props, which constitutes the classical intercolumniation, was done away. By its aid spacious interiors were covered in with vaulted ceilings of brick or stone. In return for these advantages, it demanded something more than the Grecian pillar, the upright post, calculated to resist perpendicular pressure only; it demanded, when its form was flat and its span long and low, as in a bridge, massive side-piers or abutments; and when higher and sharper, as in Norman and Gothic structures, it still required lateral supports, though less massive; their dimensions depending upon its precise form and upon the super-incumbent weight it was required to carry.

It is true, that the new forms thus introduced and the new necessities thence resulting might be hidden from view. A little ingenuity sufficed to cover them up with a Grecian mask. A flat, supplemental ceiling might conceal from the eye the vault above. The arch sprung from pillar to pillar, and which formed the actual support of the weight imposed upon it, might be disguised, so as to represent a horizontal architrave. And, finally, an entire line of wall, upon which rested a succession of groined arches, might be made of so massive a thickness, that all local projections, at the points of impost, would become unnecessary.

But there is no unity, no truth, no intrinsic integrity, and therefore no element of permanence, no living energy, in such a system. It is based upon false appearances, and cannot endure. Out of it can spring only temporary and unstable combinations; an Architecture of transition.

It offends, not only against that principle of utility, which lies at the base of just taste; but directly against an important law of beauty in Architecture. Even the uncultivated eye finds pleasure in the display of constructive relations. When a noble task is achieved, it pleases us to perceive, at a glance, how it is done. When the long cathedral aisle is covered in, securely and gracefully, by its lofty vault, it gratifies the eye and the mind to trace to their distant summit the converging lines of

Renwick Arch.t

Ackermans lith 120 Fulton S.t N.Y.

INTERIOR OF GRACE CHURCH, NEW YORK.

that vault, to distinguish the ribs that mark the curves of its groinings; to follow, down to their respective points of impost, its numerous arches; each member distinctly visible, their mechanical connection manifest and avowed, and the distribution of weights and thrusts thence resulting palpable and self-explaining.

And so also in regard to the external features essentially belonging to the arch, and exhibiting the partition of support which grows out of its structure. Its evident lateral pressure should be met by as evident lateral resistance. This is obtained in the buttress. The eye rests with satisfaction upon its long, aspiring lines, slanting upwards against the wall it strengthens; because its form and position proclaim its office. The mind recognizes in it, at once, an agent of solidity and security. There is an intuitive perception of its fitness and utility; and such a perception is always welcome and agreeable.

But these rational elements of beauty are disregarded, when we press into a foreign service, without regard to place or purpose, as did the Romans, the column of the post and lintel manner. In the hands of superficial architects, who studied forms and neglected principles, whose low ambition, never stirred by the creative energy of genius, was satisfied to imitate and adopt and combine; in such feeble hands, the majestic shaft of the Grecian colonnade was degraded from its original independence, to the station of a mere parasitical ornament; attached, for example, to the face of piers; the piers themselves being the true supports of the intervening arches.

Then followed a host of perversions; columns stilted on pedestals, or mounted, in tiers, on each other; some seeming to rest only on a paltry bracket, others bearing nothing but a meaningless finial; pediments without roofs to terminate, and entablatures with no eaves to support; entablatures broken into fragments or tortured into curves; arches imposed on fragmental cornices, or springing from amputated pilaster-heads; these and a hundred other similar incongruities are among the aberrations of this hybrid school.

That this school has won, and even yet retains, much favor, is attributable to the fact, that, among a number of tame and feeble imitators, it has numbered some architects of undoubted taste, and one or two of talent so commanding, that their works have obtained a world-wide reputation, despite the inherent defects and incongruities of the manner in which they were content to design. In England, Wren and Inigo Jones; on the European Continent, Bramante, and Michael Angelo, and Vinola, have done what skill and fertility of resource could do, for an Architecture of transition. The genius of Palladio labored in the same field, although he professed, as a disciple of Vitruvius, to fall back upon older models, and assimilated his designs somewhat more closely than did Roman architects, to the classical standard.

Very far, however, from that standard did some of these masters wander, even in

7

their best compositions. The horizontal principle they seem to have set at defiance; and even to have tasked their ingenuity to break up their principal elevations, sometimes in the most unmeaning and gratuitous manner, until everything like grandeur of mass or graceful simplicity of form was frittered away beneath petty detail. Ornament enough there was, even lavishly bestowed; columns and pilasters of every order, Roman or Grecian; door and window dressings elaborately decorated; rich friezes, sometimes swelled or pillowed; cornices very classically proportioned, and often very unclassically placed; crowning balustrades dotted with statues; in a word, sumptuous accessories in profusion; such as will always mislead and dazzle the uncultivated taste.

Some of the aberrations of this school are of an unpardonable character. In Inigo Jones' designs for a palace at Whitehall (of which, however, the banquetting hall alone was actually executed) occurs a circular court, adorned externally with two rows of human figures (Persians and Caryatides) arranged in perpendicular lines, one figure immediately above the other, with a narrow, projecting slip of entablature set upright upon the head of each; and, above these again, in the same vertical line, statues perched on the pedestals of the surmounting balustrade. The incidental enrichments are well managed, as by Jones they almost always are; yet the whole arrangement involuntarily reminds one of a set of circus tumblers mounted on each other's shoulders.

There is, without doubt, much of redeeming in some of Jones' simpler designs. Yet he and others whose talents deserved a better field, failed to give vigor and vitality to a manner essentially barren and lifeless. St. Paul's, and its far more magnificent continental rival, St. Peter's, must always be considered noble and impressive creations. But so are the Pyramids, and so are the caves of Ellora. Piles so vast as these two world-famed churches, if only the main outline be good and the general combination skilful, can hardly fail of effect; especially in a location so grand, and surrounded by accessories so imposing, as is the Roman basilica. All this is no proof either that the details are pure or the manner happy.

Design by Inigo Jones.

The dome, that feature to which these and other Roman structures owe much of their impressive character, is always costly and seldom of strict utility. In rooms designed for public speaking, it is, if of any considerable altitude, highly detrimental. The lofty semi-dome over the Hall of Representatives in the Capitol, aided, perhaps, by the recesses containing its galleries, has rendered that magnificent chamber as unfit for the purposes to which it is put, as human ingenuity could well succeed in making it.* In a general way, the dome, as a prominent feature, comports ill with the internal adaptations of any modern edifice, public or private.

I am speaking here of Roman Architecture as a distinctive school, laying claim to independence, to the merit of original conception, of truthfulness, of unity, harmony, significancy. And, as a separate school, I deny its claims to these. But, that it has often given birth to tasteful and agreeable combinations, no one acquainted with its productions will deny. Our own Capitol, especially its noble eastern front, is a favorable example.

The circular temple of Roman Architecture, (of which the only Grecian prototype is the small choragic monument of Lysicrates,) has, in some situations, a striking

---

* The consequences of so gross an error in architectural adaptation as this, are much more grave than may at first appear. They must, indeed, suggest themselves, with greater or less force, to all spectators who visit the galleries of the Chamber referred to. But one must have been, as the writer was, a member of that body for years, fully to appreciate the extent of the evil. Not the manner only, but the very spirit and tone of debate in the House of Representatives, is essentially and injuriously influenced by the form of the hall in which its members speak and listen. Noisy declamation seems in place among its resonant echoes. A calm, deliberate argument, addressed to the dispassionate reason, if not wholly swallowed up amid its vortex of sounds, appears as much out of character there as if it were delivered in an open cattle-market. Nor is this all. Half the business transacted by what in courtesy is called a deliberative body, passes wholly unnoticed by a large majority of members, from a sheer impossibility to hear, from their seats, what is going on.

This is a remarkable example of the influence—it were hardly using too strong a word to say, the *demoralizing* influence—exerted upon a legislative assembly by a mere blunder in construction. I know of no effectual remedy for it, except the construction of a new Hall of Representatives. One could be conveniently obtained at a moderate cost, by carrying forward the eastern portico and steps of the Capitol, about ninety feet, so as to permit the interposition, between them and the main building, of a projection similar to that on the west front. The Capitol, which now presents, if viewed from the north or south, a lopsided appearance, would then assume the form of a Greek cross.

This proposal (first suggested, I believe, by Mr. Robert Mills, formerly public architect) will be better understood by an inspection of the annexed diagrams.

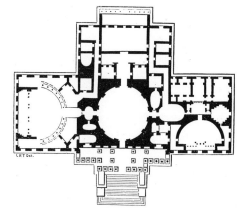

Capitol as it is.

The first presents a ground-plan of the Capitol as it is; *a*, being the Representatives' Hall; *b*, the Senate Chamber; *c*, the Library of Congress; *d*, the Rotunda, and *e*, the eastern portico.

The next cut shows the Capitol, with the proposed addition; *a*, being the new Hall, interposed between the main building and the central portico and steps on the eastern front; *b*, as before,

effect. Of this the most picturesque example, perhaps, is the temple of the Sybil, at Tivoli.*

Of one of its styles, usually known as the Italian, the General Post Office, at Washington, is a graceful example, creditable to the architect who designed it. It may be considered Palladian in its general character, but is simpler than most of the Vicentine's designs. Indeed, not a few of the modern followers of Palladio, especially in England, seem to me, even if they have failed to surpass the best effects of the master they followed, to have avoided many of the blemishes which disfigure his works.†

Yet this edifice, graceful though it be, is marked, not the less, with some of the inherent defects of the Roman manner. The ground-plan of its principal front exhibits the Grecian column, fitted to stand alone and eminently appropriate in

the Senate Chamber; *d*, the Rotunda; *c*, the present Hall of Representatives; *e*, the eastern portico, and *g*, the present Library.

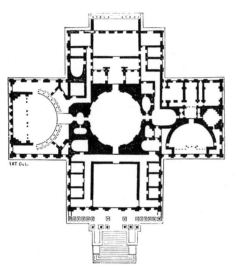

Capitol, with proposed Addition.

A mere inspection of these two ground-plans will satisfy any one who has given attention to the sources of architectural effect, that the appearance of the Capitol would be much improved by the addition suggested.

The new Hall should be finished in a plain manner, perhaps with pilasters to correspond with the style of the building; but without gallery-recesses or a sound-absorbing dome. The height of its ceiling should not exceed forty feet, the height of the new English Houses of Parliament, instead of sixty, that of the present Chamber; and its galleries, projecting, might be supported on slender iron columns, as in the Senate Chamber.

By such an addition to the Capitol, other important objects beyond the reformation of the Representatives' Hall would be gained. The present Library Room is too small for the books already placed there; and the Supreme Court Room is a dark and damp basement, ill adapted for the accommodation either of the Court or of spectators. The Library might be moved into the present Hall; and would not increase, in another century, so as to overfill it; while the present Library Room, with its alcoves removed, would give a handsome chamber, thirty-four feet by ninety-two, from which a clerk's office or other apartment could be cut at each end, and still leave ample space for a Supreme Court Room. Or, as the present Senate Chamber is gradually becoming too small for the increasing number of its members, the Library might furnish a Senate Chamber, and that now occupied as such, be ceded to the Supreme Court.

* It is given in the vignette, at the close of this chapter, from one of the illustrations of Rogers' Italy.

† I record the impression, strongly made upon me by Palladio's designs, as collected and published by his admirers. Yet I confess my doubts, whether, by an actual inspection of that master's works, on the spot where they had birth, in his own Vicenza; executed in Italian marble, its tints mellowed by time; lighted by an Italian sky; the Genius of the Place breathing over them his blinding spell; one's judgment might not be biased, or bribed, to a more favorable opinion. I have never travelled in Italy further south than Milan.

The true question, however, is independent of all local associations; since, when a style is transplanted, these are left behind.

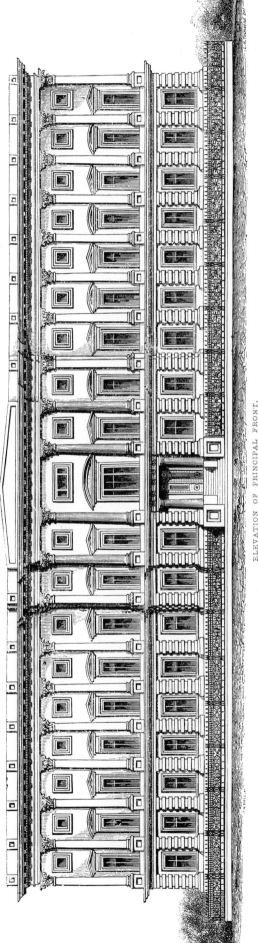

ELEVATION OF PRINCIPAL FRONT.

PART OF GROUND-PLAN, SHOWING PRINCIPAL FRONT.

GENERAL POST OFFICE, WASHINGTON.

the isolated station which Grecian
to the wall, and becoming *engaged*,

architects assigned to it, drawn up
as the phrase is; that is, sunk to
a quarter or a half of its diameter in the wall face: while, as
shown in the elevation, the *antæ*
of the old temple are repeated
between window and window;
both column and pilaster being
put to no apparent use, except to
support a slip of entablature shot
forth, for the purpose; an arrangement to which, in a previous
chapter, I have stated the objections.

Of this Italian or Palladian
style, the Library of St. Mark,
at Venice, of which a portion is
here figured, is a rich and showy
specimen. It was erected about
the middle of the sixteenth century, by Sansovino, an architect
of distinguished reputation in his
day; and exhibits the elaborate
enrichments, often managed with
delicacy and taste, which characterize some varieties of this manner. It exhibits, equally, the
characteristic vices of the hybrid
school; the pedestal; the engaged column attached to the
pier face, cutting through an
entablature, and of no essential
use as a support; the arch
springing from a classical cornice; the surmounting of one
order by another, and of both by
a crowning balustrade. Brilliant
as is the effect, the manner is
inherently faulty. There is nei-

ther breadth of mass, nor simple grace of outline. The entire elevation is cut up by incidental decoration. There is no truth of constructive expression. The horizontal principle is violated, yet it is not replaced by the vertical.*

There is, however, a variety of the Italian style, which cannot be properly included under Roman Architecture, and against which the above objections cannot be urged. It is the Palatial style of Italy; in which pilasters and engaged columns are discarded, and the architect trusts for his effects chiefly to the dressings of doors and windows, and to rich, bold weather-mouldings. This style, skillfully managed, particularly in edifices of great size and unbroken fronts, produces an agreeable and harmonious impression. It is, in my judgment, worthy of more attention than modern architects have usually bestowed upon it. But, like the other varieties of Italian, it is costly; demanding, for its best effects, materials and workmanship both of an expensive character; marble, with smooth finish and carefully sculptured enrichments.†

Of this variety, sometimes termed *astylar*, the Farnese Palace, at Rome, may be cited as a good example. So, also, but on a smaller scale, is the Pandolfini Palace, at Florence, ascribed to Raphael, and which furnished to Barry the general idea of his "Travellers' Club House," Pall Mall, London.‡

In its interior adaptations, as in its external features, Roman Architecture exhibits some happy combinations and many striking defects. Several good Roman interiors may be seen in the Capitol; perhaps the best is the room east of that assigned to the Vice President, and immediately adjoining it. The interior of a church in New York, (St. Paul's, near the Astor House,) supplies a notable example of hybrid incongruities; managed, too, with some skill, and with all the advantage to be derived from classical accuracy in details.

---

* In street architecture, this Italian style, well managed, often shows to more advantage than other manners, intrinsically more meritorious. Stewart's marble building, in New York, may be cited in proof. Its front on Broadway has not often, in its way, been surpassed.

† The entablature around the General Post Office, though devoid of superfluous enrichment, cost *fifty dollars* per running foot. Had this style been selected for the Smithsonian edifice, and had a similar cornice been adopted, its cost, for the north and south fronts of the main building alone, would have exceeded *twenty thousand dollars*. The heavy corbel-course which forms the actual weather-moulding of that building, cost but *seven dollars* per running foot; less than *three thousand dollars* in all. The difference in material is, of course, an important item.

‡ A description of this edifice, one of the prettiest Italian buildings of modern times, may be found in a volume entitled the "Travellers' Club House," published by Weale, in 1839. The illustrations are very carefully executed, and give, not only the general elevations, but the minute details of the design. The English architect has, I think, improved upon the Florentine original. The street front resembles that of the Palazzo Pandolfini; but the rear elevation, managed with much taste, is, so far as I know, original. The details, throughout, are marked with great purity and grace, and may furnish, to street architects, a valuable study. As in the case of all highly finished Italian buildings, the expense of its erection was considerable. With a street front of about seventy-two feet, a depth of about a hundred and two, and but two stories high, it cost, exclusive of fittings and furniture, nearly one hundred and thirteen thousand dollars.

The gallery columns are each surmounted by isolated portions of entablature; and from the summit of each fragmental cornice a groined arch springs; while the points of impost for these arches along the walls are also portions of projecting entablature, terminating below in a scroll, or console. The composition is bad. It exhibits no unity, no calculated, harmonious relation of parts. The column and the arch, each in itself a graceful feature, are

St. Paul's, New York.

paired, not matched. The square fragment of entablature, with its broad-brimmed summit, joins but does not connect them. It has an obtrusive, top-heavy air. It is a piece of misplaced finery. It never would have been thought of in such a form, as a short, square, heavy-corniced post, stilted on a circular column, if the architect had not been haunted by the continuous entablature of a Corinthian colonnade, and sought to reproduce its details, in a connection in which there was, and could be, essentially, no entablature whatever.

If this mode of impost be compared with that in the Baptistery of Pisa,* the superior propriety and grace of the latter will be readily perceived.

But it is in the best Norman or Gothic interiors alone that complete correspondence is found, between supporting props below and arches or a vaulted ceiling above.† The shaft of the clustered pillar has a special adaptation for arching or vaulting.

Corhampton, Hants.

* See Chapter IV. of this work.

† It was by very gradual steps that this harmonious correspondence of parts in Arch Architecture was reached. In the succeeding chapter I shall have occasion to speak of the heavy and over-massive and inharmonious character of the early Norman style. If we go further back, to Saxon examples, we shall find the adaptations still more rude and clumsy, as instanced in the accompanying sketch of a Saxon impost, from Corhampton, England. Rude and clumsy, however, as it is, it is less studiously incongruous than the hybrid example from St. Paul's; and, so far, it may be considered preferable to it.

Grace Church, New York.

A portion of these mouldings, after running up in perpendicular lines to the pillar capital, spring again, from the summit of that capital, similar in character and form, and constitute the mouldings, for example, of side-aisle arches, while others, cutting clear through the capital, ascend into clerestories, there to become vaulting-shafts, from the caps of which, as an impost, spring ribs for groining.* In either case the eye follows, with satisfaction, the long, ascending lines of the mouldings, which thus connect and identify, as a specially adapted and harmonious whole, the pillar that supports, and the arch or vault that is supported. No corresponding idea of unity or fitness is suggested by the arrangement of the interior of St. Paul's, as heretofore figured.

Again, if we compare the Roman bracket employed in the above example from St. Paul's interior, with the Norman or Gothic corbel, we cannot, I think, hesitate a moment in giving our preference to the latter, both as a more graceful feature, and as a more fitting impost, whence to spring an arch.

The same church of St. Paul's furnishes one of the

* The cut above, representing a portion of the interior of Grace Church, New York, exhibits the arrangement here alluded to. See, also, in this connection, the general view of the interior of the same church, given in a preceding part of this chapter. Compare, further, with these, a Norman interior figured in the next chapter.

Bracket, St. Paul's, New York.

Corbel, Smithsonian Institution.

best examples to be found in this or perhaps in any other country, of the Roman style, adapted to spire Architecture. Indeed, it is not often that one meets, in any

St. Paul's, New York.

style, with a spire of its size producing a better effect.* That effect is greatly improved by the *battering*, or inward slope, of its columns, giving to the structure that beautiful pyramidal outline, which imparts to the finest Gothic spires much of the charm they possess.

* The general idea of this edifice is derived from the church of St. Martin in the Fields, London. But the spire as much exceeds in grace of design the English original, as the straggling, four-column portico on Broadway falls short of that, supported on six columns, from which it is copied. The position of the spire in the New York church is much more judicious than in St. Martin's. In the latter it immediately surmounts, and overpowers, the front portico ; while in the former it is placed, as it should be, in the rear of the building.

Roman spires, as usually designed and placed, are, for the most part, unsightly features. I prefer the Italian Campanile.

The chief advantage which the Gothic spire possesses over the Roman, thus skill-fully managed, is the greater size which, without undue multiplication of its main divisions, the former can attain, and the longer, more continuous sweep of its upward lines. A comparison may be instituted by examining that of the Hotel de Ville at Brussels, one among the noblest specimens of the Gothic spire in the world.

Compare, again, with these, a French example of a later phase of hybrid Architecture, the "Clock Tower" at Mons, figured on the opposite page. It illustrates that whimsical style, succeeding the Gothic, and which, deriving its name from the date of its first appearance (the fifteenth century,) has been termed the *Cinque-cento*. The ascending lines are all arrested and lost. Features hetero-geneous and discordant are brought together. Oriental ornament surmounts Roman details. The manner is capricious and degenerate. It will not bear comparison, for a moment, with that of either of the two previous examples.

And here let me beg those who may have fol-lowed, thus far, these strictures on what I have called a hybrid style, to bear in mind, that this brief treatise regards public, not domestic, Archi-tecture; and that even as regards public Architec-ture, most of its remarks apply only in those cases, in which the taste of the architect, or the ambition of those who direct his labors, may have decided to overstep the line of rigid utility, and to stamp upon the structures they are charged to erect, more or less of embellishing ornament and distinctive character.

Hotel de Ville, Brussels.

In the construction of private dwellings, with rooms and openings of ordinary size, the arch, except perhaps in vaulting the cellar, is seldom em-ployed. Room ceilings, as well as door and window-heads, are usually flat. In such a plan of construction the pressure exerted on the walls of the dwelling is, as in ancient Grecian Architecture, perpendicular only.   There are no points of impost where a powerful side-thrust must be met and resisted.   Heavy buttresses, then, are not demanded.

The Grecian column, with its cornice, or its entire entablature, cannot be considered incongruous to such a mode of con-struction, in which the post and lintel principle is preserved, and the horizontal line predominates.   A Grecian portico, for example, with classical pillars and pediment, em-ployed to mark and adorn the main entrance to such a dwelling, is not to be condemned as a hybrid feature. There may be other objections to it, as that it is too ambitious a deco-ration for a simple dwelling.   And this objection is strictly applicable where the columns are made of such size and height as to cross two or more stories, and the portico occu-pies an entire front.   This aping of the temple *pronaos* in front of a private residence, unless it be of princely magnificence, carries with it an air of over-pretension and in-appropriateness; to say nothing of the practical objections already alluded to on the score of light and cost.   The simple one-story porch, with a pillar, or a couple of pillars on each side, cannot be set down as obtruding or offensive.   Yet, as a strict matter of taste, I concur in a

Clock Tower, Mons, France.

suggestion I have somewhere seen made, that it is better, even then, to avoid classical pillars—to abstain from all temple reminiscences—and to content one's self, in erecting a shelter for the outer door of a plain house, with a porch supported on square, or at least rectilinear props, composed of the same material as the wall of the dwelling, and seeming, as it were, a slice or section taken from that wall. Thus, in a brick dwelling, the porch might be supported on square piers of brick; in a stone dwelling on posts of stone. Or in a brick house, of which the sills, lintels, cornice, &c., are of stone, the porch props might correspond in material. Even in the case of a frame, protected by weather-boarding, the principle might be carried out, and the porch be supported on square props of timber, perhaps weather-boarded. The suggestion has this advantage, that such porches would be features wholly devoid of pretension; they would never suggest omissions, or indicate a striving after a style beyond our reach; their effect would be simple and harmonious.

In public edifices, which should always be made fire-proof, the apartments may happen to be of such size and shape, that iron joists and girders can be conveniently employed throughout. If they are, the side-props of Gothic architecture are not superinduced; for, although, of course, the last in succession of the low, short-spanned brick arches, (usually sprung from joist to joist, and upon which the floor is laid,) finally reaches, at either side, the wall of the building; yet, in the first place, these arches are small and light, seldom of more than eight feet span, of the thickness of a single brick, and having no heavy weight superimposed; exerting, therefore, no very powerful lateral thrust: and, besides, they are of the nature of a barrel vault, abutting equally on the whole line of wall, and demanding no local projection. The introduction of classical features, in such a connection, is not obnoxious, therefore, to the charge of incongruity.

It is in those public structures, in which, as it was among the Romans, the arch is actually brought into use; in which the ceilings of spacious apartments are vaulted with brick or stone; in which the intervals between piers, jambs, or other impost-props are spanned by curved supports, whether semicircular or of pointed Gothic form; that the horizontal principle of the Greeks, its closely approached props, and its long, level entablatures, should never be affected, even if considerations of cost and convenience stand not in the way.

A notable example of a departure from this rule, is to be found in the case of a building of which the exterior presents the most elaborate example of the ancient temple ever executed on this continent; the Girard College for Orphans.

The will of Girard prescribed, that the college should be rendered fire-proof by vaulting its various apartments; whether by means of the groined or the barrel arch is not distinctly declared.* Those charged with its erection, adopted groined vaulting. Yet they decided to employ, for its exterior, the manner of the Grecian school. The

---

* The words are, that " the floors and the roof shall be of solid materials, on arches turned on proper centres, so that no wood shall be used except for doors, windows and shutters."
Groined arches were probably intended.

consequences of such a decision are detailed in the Final Report of the architect, recently published.

After stating that all the rooms and vestibules in the building are vaulted with brick; those of the basement, first and second stories, with groined arches, springing from piers four feet square, and projecting in the angles to receive the bands, he adds:

"The lateral thrust of the arches is resisted by iron bands of one inch by five inches, extending around all the rooms and vestibules. One of these bands is placed one foot below the spring, and another one foot above the spring, of the first and second story arches, and one immediately at the spring of those of the third story; making five complete bands around the building and through all the interior walls. Three bands of similar dimensions extend around the portico, one being bedded in each architrave moulding, and one through the frieze; cross bars are introduced between the building and the entablature. * * In order to give additional strength to the banding, diagonal bars are introduced against each groin pier, and securely riveted to the principal bands."

The whole weight of this banding, the architect informs us, is one hundred and fourteen tons, and its cost fourteen thousand four hundred dollars.

This expedient of securing, by a succession of encircling hoops, a building massive and substantial as is the Girard College, suggests, at once, some radical error in the principles of its construction. And that error consists in imposing upon an arched interior the forms of the post and lintel school. The colonnade of the Girard College, to say nothing of cost or utility, is wholly out of place. Ponderous, sumptuous as it is, it is inefficient to resist the thrust of the vaults it encloses. Girard had selected, for the interior of his building, the arched construction. Those to whom was confided the execution of his wishes, ought to have followed out the theme. It led, naturally and properly, to the side supports of the Gothic manner. The thrust of the groined arches, with the ponderous load superimposed, ought to have been met, at the proper points, by massive buttresses, weighted down, if necessary, by surmounting pinnacles. These would have supplied, at a moderate cost, that security, which a peristyle costing two-thirds of a million wholly fails to furnish. If they had been less magnificent than that peristyle, they would have been more appropriate; and the spectacle would not have been presented of a structure, calculated by the imperishable nature of its materials and the solid character of its workmanship, to set at defiance the dilapidating influence of time, hooped together, lest it fall to pieces, by a hundred and fourteen tons of iron.*

* I have no intention of asserting the opinion, that had Girard lived to erect his own College, he would have avoided the error in construction into which those charged with the execution of his will have fallen; though, doubtless, he would have carried out that error after a far less expensive fashion. It is, indeed,

I know of no circumstances under which a spacious vaulted structure can be clothed, fittingly or advantageously, under the forms of the classical school.   Such a manner imposed upon an edifice with far-reaching arched supports, can be introduced only by masking, instead of displaying, its internal structure and the mechanical relation of its parts.   The architectural language of such a style is false.   The style itself is incongruent, impure, and to be avoided; it is at variance with the principles of utility, and repugnant to the dictates of just taste.

evident, that the great merchant was a poor architect.   The idea of buttresses to arrest the spread of his groined arches had, clearly, never occurred to him; for though there has been employed, in hooping together the College, some eight or ten times as much iron as he considered necessary, yet he did deem it proper to instruct, that, at the point whence the arches of each story sprung, "a chain composed of bars of inch square iron, each bar about ten feet long, and linked together by hooks formed of the ends of the bars, shall be laid straightly and horizontally along the several walls, and shall be as tightly as possible worked into the centre of them throughout;" and this " to prevent cracking or swerving in any part."

Such a provision (albeit wholly insufficient for security in the present case, unless aided by buttresses,) was calculated to mislead from the manner of construction proper for vaulted buildings; although, even in some Gothic edifices, when undue lightness of structure was affected, iron banding, in aid of buttresses, has been employed.

In condemning, then, that error in construction which indued with a Grecian exterior an extensive arched edifice, I cast no especial blame on the executors of Girard's will.   The error committed was one evidently shared by the founder himself.

Temple of the Sybil, Tivoli.

Upjohn Arch.

CHURCH OF THE HOLY COMMUNION, NEW YORK.

CHAPTER VI.

OF ARCH ARCHITECTURE.

"In these exquisite examples, (Norman and Gothic,) we observe all constructive necessities not only provided, but boldly shown; not only shown, but made advantageous to pictorial effect; not rendered merely endurable to the eye by decoration, but giving an enviable opportunity for decoration : not, in fine, hypocritical examples of the Iago school, "I am not what I am," but honest and eloquent creatures, begotten of science and of taste, and proclaiming the why and wherefore of their being."

LOUDON'S ARCHITECTURAL MAGAZINE.

> "The darkened roof rose high aloof,
>   On pillars lofty and light and small;
> The keystone that locked each ribbed aisle
> Was a fleur-de-lis or or a quatre-feuille;
> The corbels were carved, grotesque and grim,
> And the pillars, with clustered shafts so trim,
> With base and with capital flourished around,
> Seemed bundles of lances which garlands had bound."

SCOTT'S LAY.

I confess my predilections for Arch Architecture. I like its truth, its candor, its boldness. I like its lofty character, its aspiring lines. I like the independence with which it has shaken off the shackles of formal rule, and refused obedience to the despotic laws of monotonous repetition. I like its changeful aspects, the infinite succession of its forms, the endless variety of character in its expressions.

At times, indeed, its boldness has run into temerity, and its freedom degenerated into license. The whimsical and the grotesque have, not unfrequently, disfigured its earlier productions; and, of its later ones, some have been wantonly pushed to the extreme of architectural possibility; while, in others, the marked and simpler forms of an earlier and more vigorous era have been so laboriously obscured by a fanciful network of stone, so overloaded by a lavish profusion of ornamental details*—of tracery and fretting and tabernacle work; of cusps and featherings and crocketings and pinnacles and finials and niches and canopies and pendants—that the edifice

---

* It is not my intention to deny, that, with all its faulty profusion of ornament, late Gothic has also its redeeming beauties. There are some, even of the richest details of the latest styles, which, it must be

became a confused mass of indiscriminate enrichment; and all firm and graceful outline was lost under the intricate mazes of gorgeous decoration.

But these aberrations of a luxurious and degenerate taste are incidental and extraneous only, not essential and inherent. They are adventitious excrescences, that have attached themselves to a noble and healthy tree, of which they form no vital portion, and from which they can be readily and advantageously detached.

For the Architecture itself, apart from these disfiguring effeminacies, and in its simpler and purer phase, after the rude and clumsy of the Saxon era had disappeared, and before the gaudy

Main Entrance, Cathedral of Troyes, France.

and fantastical of the fifteenth century had supervened, it seems to me to compare with the classical model, as does the bold and quaint and effective and lofty and spirit-stirring Saxon of Shakspeare, with the smooth and polished and sonorous and formally elegant Latin of Cicero.

The prejudices which some entertain

Cloisters, Gloucester Cathedral.

confessed, are graceful and effective; for example, what is called *fan tracery* vaulting, occurring in late perpendicular work, and only, I believe, in English examples. An idea of its effect may be obtained from the annexed cut. It is too elaborate and expensive to merit adoption among us.

against any style but the strictly uniform, are easily vanquished. A little habit not only reconciles the eye to the irregular variety of Gothic, but causes it to be sought for and esteemed far beyond the rigidly formal. Even in street Architecture, its effects are happy and striking. Take an example from the ancient provincial city of Bourges, the same in which the celebrated Condé spent his early school-days;

House of Jacques Cœur, Bourges.*

the mansion of Jacques Cœur, on the old Gothic balustrade of which, as a modern essayist has suggested, the great Captain may have read, and adopted as his own, the inspiriting motto,

" A vaillants Cœurs, rien impossible."

But it is not the attractive exterior, striking as it is; not the picturesque beauty, which characterizes alike its boldest outlines and its most delicate details; nor yet the pictorial effects, varying with every changeful aspect, which the rich variety of its irregular masses successively present; it is not these, which chiefly influence my preference for Arch Architecture. That preference is mainly founded on considerations more prosaic and practical. That same picturesque irregularity which pleases the eye and charms the fancy, is an important feature in an Archi-

tecture that is to satisfy modern wants. The flexibility which the Norman and Gothic manners possess; the facility with which they assume whatever external forms may be suggested by interior purpose; the easy freedom with which they lend themselves, as occasion arises, to amendment or addition; all these are essential conditions, in an Architecture that is to secure lasting favor among us: all these are essential charac-

* Those who prefer a little more regularity than this cut presents, may obtain it in such examples as that

teristics in an Architecture that is to attain, in our utilitarian age and in our matter-of-fact country, to the character of national.

For the minor irregularities of enrichment which characterize the Arch Architecture of the Middle Ages, as the endless variety of detail often presented by a series of corbels, or capitals, or bosses, having the same general shape and size and appearance at a distance, and of which the variations are detected only by closer inspection, there is not the same substantial reason to be offered.   Yet these encroachments on the settled uniformity of classical examples, give, I think, to the Arch manner, additional interest and attraction.   If, at Athens in the days of her splendor, we had visited that temple of Jupiter Olympius, upon which generation after generation had expended labor and treasure, before it stood, at last, the sumptuous monument of art

of the Hotel de Ville, (in other words, the Town-hall,) at St. Quentin, here figured.   It would be difficult to find a prettier design for shop fronts.   And if a strict copy give us too much of ornament, the general outline might be preserved, with happy effect.

Hotel de Ville, St. Quentin, France.

The old Town-halls of the European Continent, those especially in Belgium, furnish examples of a variety of Gothic, well suited, under many circumstances, to the public buildings of a city.

it was, its first aspect must have seemed to us impressive and imposing in the highest degree.   Yet, after we had inspected one of the fluted shafts, of which a hundred and twenty-four rose from its marble stylobate; after we had examined one of the rich capitals that crowned that forest of columns; we had inspected and examined them all.   Each of these magnificent capitals, even down to the minutest line of an acanthus leaf or the slightest curve of a volute, was a copy, exact, unvarying, scrupulously reproduced, of its neighbor.   And so of the next, and the next, and the next, throughout all that gorgeous peristyle.   A hundred and twenty-four times the same identical conception was repeated.

Not thus is it that Nature labors.   No leaf in the forest that is a servile copy of its fellow.   And though man, in his works, can never attain her infinite variety, he need not, at vast pains and cost, task his ingenuity to depart, as widely as possible, from her example.   "Is it less tautology," asks a modern writer, "to describe a thing over and over again with lines, than it is with words?"   The remark was applied to Painting; but has it not its application to Architecture also?

Other considerations recommend this school of Architecture for public edifices. Its economy, in materials and in workmanship; the facilities it affords, beyond the temple model, for warming and ventilating; and, yet more especially, the advantages it possesses over older styles, whether Grecian or Roman, in its system of fenestration.

A diagram, suggested by a very original thinker,* may serve to illustrate this last remark, and to exhibit, in a general way, the marked difference between Roman and Gothic interiors.

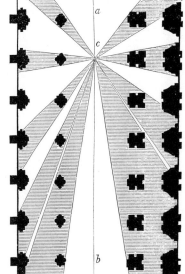

It represents the ground-plan of a church, or other public building of similar arrangement, divided by the line *a b*, longitudinally into two equal parts.   On the one side it is distributed and proportioned as in a Gothic Cathedral, to wit, that of Amiens; on the other as in the Roman Church of St. Paul's; the pillars, piers, walls and window openings being laid down in their relative proportions, as they actually occur in these two buildings.

A mere inspection of the diagram will supply a pretty accurate idea of the contrast in style, as to lightness and airiness, of the respective interiors.

The actual depth of wall in the Gothic plan, including buttresses, is as great as in the Roman; but the arrangement in the former is such, (resembling a succession of short walls or deep piers set at right angles to the

* Dr. James Anderson, in his "Origin, Excellencies and Defects of Grecian and Gothic Architecture."

main line of the building,) as to permit wider interstices, or in other words more spacious windows, without risk to the solidity of the structure.

It is not, however, alone the greater size of window that gives advantage to Gothic fenestration. The lightness of Gothic pillars as compared with Roman piers, is an important item in the case. To a spectator at *c*, as the lines of shading prove, in the Roman Church but *two* out of seven windows would be visible; while in the Gothic Cathedral *five* out of the seven would come distinctly into view.

As regards the various styles of Arch Architecture, the Moorish, Arabian or Sara-

Moorish Interior, in Mosque at Cordova, Spain.

cenic variety, with its many-cusped arches, and its light fantastic forms, and its Persian lattice-work, and its rich mosaics, has not manly vigor nor sterling principle enough,

to bring it into general use or favor. Some of its examples are tasteful and elegant, and many of its airy and graceful details may supply good models, or profitable hints, to the architect wherever iron is extensively introduced among materials for construction: but Eastern genius never fairly penetrated to the first principles of the style in which it worked. The proof is, that in Arabian Architecture there is no persistive prevalence of that vertical principle, the purest and most essential element of Arch Architecture, and which, in the hands of Gothic builders, became so happy and pregnant a theme. To the last, Moorish edifices showed the horizontal lines of the Grecian manner; even in examples erected so near the fountain head of the Gothic as in the island of Sicily.

Mosque at Cordova, Spain.

The Norman, and the Gothic, of various ages, belong, in my opinion, to a much better and purer school.   The exact periods which mark the boundaries of the principal varieties of that school are somewhat variously stated by different writers. Commencing with the Norman conquest, (that is, in the latter half of the eleventh century,) they ran through four or five centuries; of which (to speak with approximating accuracy and in a form to be readily remembered) the Norman may be said to have occupied one, and each of the chief divisions of Gothic one also: though each, of course, somewhat encroached, before the change of style became complete, on the next.* The Perpendicular,† however, of which a continental variety is usually termed Flamboyant,‡ continued to drag out a lingering existence, gradually declining in vigor and purity, for three-quarters of a century longer; encroached on, in England, at the close of the fifteenth century, by the Elizabethan,§ with

St. Peter's, Louvain.

* To speak with somewhat greater accuracy, the dates of their respective duration are usually set down, by the best English authorities, as follows :

    Norman, Lombard, or Rounded, (in English examples,)   .   .   .   from 1066 to 1190.
    Gothic, or Pointed, three varieties, viz :
        1. Early English, or Lancet, ...   from 1190 to 1300.
        2. Decorated, ...   from 1300 to 1390.
        3. Perpendicular, or Florid, ...   from 1390 to 1550.

† The term is derived from the vertical lines which occur in its window tracery, and become one of its distinguishing characteristics. An English example, from All Saints' Church, Maidstone, illustrates this.

‡ So called from the flame-like wavings of its window tracery; of which the effect may be judged from the cut above, exhibiting a handsome French specimen of Flamboyant tracery, from a cathedral in Louvain.

§ The Tudor style, an indefinite term, is sometimes made to include the Elizabethan, sometimes restricted to late Perpendicular. In the Elizabethan, the pointed arch became gradually flattened, until its principle and very form were gone. The details of this style closely resemble those of the Cinque-cento.

All Saints'. Maidstone.

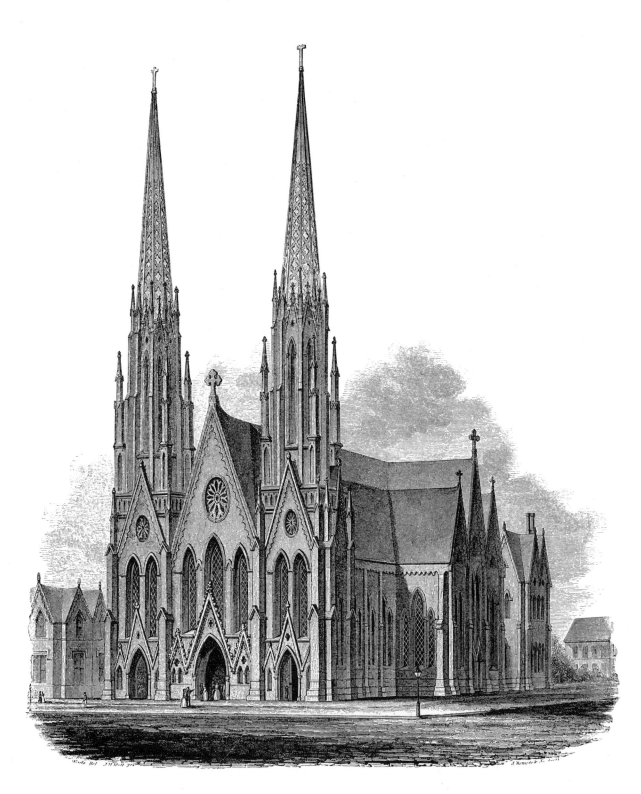

CALVARY CHURCH,

FROM THE FOURTH AVENUE, NEW-YORK.

its depressed and bastard arches and its whimsical details, and, on the European Continent, by the minute Cinque-cento.   These were the first phases of that so-called revived classical style, (termed in France *de la Renaissance,*) which finally swept before it the whole system of pointed forms, and usurped its place.   It was greatly aided, in so doing, by the disgrace and downfall of the society of Free-masons, and the consequent loss, to the Architecture of those days, of that practical science and constructive skill, essential to the bold designs of the Gothic school, and which was then in the almost exclusive possession of that powerful body; seeming, in a measure and for the time, to perish with them.

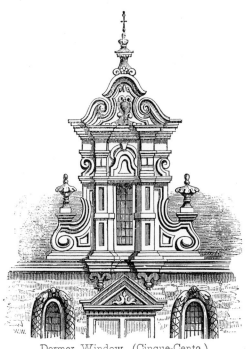

Dormer Window, (Cinque-Cento,)
Beguinage, Brussels.

We have already among us (and the number is daily increasing) examples more or less pure of the Norman and of the several periods of Gothic. New York, in this, seems to have taken the lead.   In that city, the Church of St. George and that of the Puritans are examples of the later Norman; Calvary and the Church of the Annunciation, of the Early English, or Lancet; the Church of the Holy Communion and the South Dutch Church, of the Decorated; Trinity, of the Perpendicular; and Grace Church, of the early Flamboyant.*   Other cities are gradually following the lead.

In looking back through these various styles, both Norman and Gothic, from the birth of the former about the time of the Conquest, to the final extinction of the latter, some five centuries thereafter, I give preference to the earlier varieties.   It is in Continental Europe and Great Britain, and it is chiefly during the TWELFTH and THIRTEENTH CENTURIES, that the manner of Arch Architecture seems to me the purest and healthiest, the most worthy of study, and the most likely to furnish a point of departure, whence American genius, piloted by good taste and steering by the polar star of utility, may win honor and profit by a successful voyage into unexplored regions of art.

* Perspective views of Calvary Church, of the Church of the Holy Communion and of Grace Church are given, as specimens of New York Architecture. To the liberality of the Vestry of Grace Church the Smithsonian Institution is indebted for the two plates exhibiting the interior and exterior of that edifice. In the plate representing the Church of the Holy Communion, (Dr. Muhlenberg's,) landscape scenery has been substituted for the streets of the city, as more appropriate to the character of the building.

The two centuries above referred to embrace, as we have seen, a portion of the two great divisions of Arch Architecture; to wit, of the Lombard or Norman, and the Gothic proper; the former (in its later and lighter styles, however) occupying the greater part of the twelfth century; while through the remainder of that century and the whole of the thirteenth, the Gothic gradually developed itself; passing through

Shottesbrooke Church, Berkshire, England.

the Early English, and, before the commencement of the fourteenth century, reaching the Decorated;* this last exhibiting, to their full extent, its powers and capabilities.

* So termed by Rickman, but not with strict appropriateness; for some of its best examples are comparatively plain, as the beautiful country church of Shottesbrooke, figured above; and rich ornament is by no means an essential characteristic. It is usually considered the most completely developed variety of Gothic; and some of the noblest Gothic structures, the cathedrals of Cologne and Rheims and Amiens, for example, are in this style. The tail-piece to Chapter VII supplies an example of Decorated tracery.

As regards the merits of these two manners, the Norman with semicircular-headed openings and the pointed-arched Gothic, an absolute preference cannot, I think, be justly awarded to either. The mere form of opening, though it be the most obvious feature, and though it has, to some extent, naturally drawn after it, in either style, certain peculiarities, cannot be properly assumed as the chief point of difference.

In so far as the Lombard variety may have merited the epithet bestowed upon it by Mr. Gunn, of *Romanesque*, or debased Roman, its peculiarities are decidedly impure and objectionable. Among these may be reckoned its lingering predilections for classical forms and proportions; as for columns both in interiors and in exteriors,* bearing a clumsy resemblance to the Grecian; its reluctance, until some of its latest examples, fairly to carry out the vertical principle, as, to prolong mouldings, from clustered pillars up into clerestories or along arches; its occasional use of barrel vaulting; its propensity to provide against lateral thrust by a general thickening of wall, instead of projecting well-defined buttresses. There may be added, as objections,

Norman Interior, Rosheim.

especially to its earlier productions, that their general proportions were often short and massive, even to clumsiness, the effect being increased by a prevalence of rect-

* There are some fine old specimens of massive Norman, so picturesque in their design, that one is half

10

angular faces and square-edged projections; that its doors and windows, after the fortress fashion of the day, were too small, and too far apart, for modern purposes of light and ventilation; that it trusted, for its effects, too much to sculptured surfaces and too little to projecting members of graceful form and deep shadow: finally, as the general result of these shortcomings, that, in most

St. Michel, Pavia.

of its examples, there is a lack of unity and harmonious accordance of parts, which may be traced to some remaining want of confidence in its own powers, and hesitation in discarding precedents that were no longer appropriate.

But, on the other hand, there is much, especially in its later examples, of pure and redeeming, to offset these defects. It exhibits more mass and breadth than the true Gothic; it has more of simplicity and severity of outline; it is less cut up with adventitious and ambitious ornament; altogether, it has less air of pretension and more appearance of solidity. Its aspect is imposing, rather than ornate. Its Campaniles with an Italian look about them and its bell-towers more peculiarly Norman with their quaint outline, have a picturesque

Notre-Dame-La-Grande, Poitiers

tempted to make an exception, in their favor, to the above stricture. These are chiefly to be found on the Rhine, in Normandy, and throughout France, where the examples of this style are decidedly preferable to the English. One of the finest is a tower from the ancient Cathedral of Notre-Dame-La-Grande, in Poitiers, (the capital of Poitou, celebrated in English history;) here figured from the "Moyen Age Pittoresque." Despite the defects it illustrates, and which, in modern structures, we should abstain from copying, its effect must be admitted to be attractive and imposing.

WEST WING, SMITHSONIAN INSTITUTION;

FROM THE NORTH-EAST.

effect.   Its apse, appropriately introduced, is also an effective feature.*   Its windows, with their simple, semicircular heads, surmounted by a plain label or sometimes merely splayed, and devoid of elaborate tracery† or feathering, have an air of substantial grace.   So have its doors, when not overloaded with enrichment. With the same variety as the Gothic, it has fewer members and less complication of details.   Its entire expression is less ostentatious, and, if political character may be ascribed to Architecture, more republican.

Library Window,
Smithsonian Institution.

Its rival and successor, the Gothic, shows, even in its earlier style, greater self-reliance, and a character more distinctive and matured. Its architects were better workmen, more deeply read in the mysteries of pressure and counter-pressure, more skillful in the arts of mechanical construction. There was, in a general way, more originality and consistency in their designs, and more freedom and confi-

Window in
Campanile.

dence in their execution.   There was a more direct and distinct stamping of external feature by the agency of internal shape and purpose.   Constructive relations were more openly proclaimed.   And the forms thence resulting were found to lend themselves to occasion for ornament with a facility so enticing, that it is little wonder if the spirit of a rude age, ever attracted by the dazzling and delighted with display, caught eagerly at the tempting opportunity, and caused enrichment to be carried beyond the limits of reason and just taste.

This result was greatly hastened, also, by the circumstance, that the public Architecture of that age, as among the Greeks, was chiefly of an ecclesiastical character;

* The *Apse*, a common feature both in Norman and Gothic Architecture, usually occurs in the form of a semicircular, or polygonal projection, terminating the choir or aisles of a church, or sometimes its transepts.   An example of the semicircular Apse, the form chiefly employed in the Norman style, may be seen in St. George's Church, New York.   Another is given, in connection with a single Campanile, in the annexed view, taken from the north-east, of the west wing of the Smithsonian Institution.   Of the double Campanile an example has already been figured, in Chapter II.   The small window figured above, to illustrate the effects of a simple splay, is from this Campanile.

† The great majority of Norman windows, except they be circular, are wholly without tracery.   There are examples, however, to the contrary, chiefly in Italy : one of these is met with in the semicircular-headed arcades of the Campo Santo, at Pisa, where the tracery is Gothic in its character.   An example of simple tracery, appropriate to the Norman manner, is to be found in the Museum windows of the Smithsonian building, one of which is figured in a subsequent part of this chapter.

and that its efforts were directed by a body of men such as the world has seldom seen; unbounded in ambition, wonderful in resource,

> " Who, with the terrors of Futurity,
> Mingled whate'er enchants and fascinates,
> Music and painting, sculpture, rhetoric,
> And dazzling light and darkness visible,
> And architectural pomp, such as none else!"

In the system of the Catholic hierarchy, imposing magnificence was a calculated agency. The fraternity of Freemasons, if they were not actually sent forth from Italy into Northern Europe, on an architectural mission, by the Roman Pontiff, travelled, at least, with safe-conducts from under his hand, and with letters of credence and recommendation, bearing the pontifical signature.

The natural result, to the Architecture of the Middle Ages, was, that its influences came to be studied with a view rather to take captive the imagination, than to conciliate the judgment; that the grand and the daring were sought after, more than the harmonious and the appropriate; that the more legitimate effects produced by gracefulness of outline, and happy management of light and shade from bold projecting members, and just proportions, and artistical grouping of masses, and skillful handling of naturally suggested details, were, after a time, cast into comparative neglect, by the overshadowing influence of a growing taste for pomp and magnificence.

In the end, too, as men will carry even the best principles to extremes, the vertical element itself, that had so happily guided the first efforts of the Gothic school, was run into absolute extravagance. Higher and higher the sacred structures rose, each architect inspired by the ambition to overtop the work of his predecessors. Ever more slender and tall and sharp became the forms, stretching up beyond the habitations of men, and far above all edifices constructed for secular purposes; ever closer were approached the gigantic piers; ever narrower and loftier were made the interstices; until, at last, the very figures in these waxed lank and wire-drawn, as the only condition on which they might retain their places in the high, narrow bays and niches, which the proximity of pillars and mullions permitted to exist between them.

Without according, then, either to the Norman or Gothic manner, an absolute preference, I venture the opinion, that among the later specimens of the·first and the earlier examples of the second, there is better promise of material out of which to erect for America a national style of Architecture, than among the monuments of any other style now extant.

But as a servile copy of manners is never happy or pleasing, so is it also in Architecture. "The letter killeth, but the spirit giveth life." If the mere copying, with unquestioning fidelity, of any models, even the best selected, sufficed to impart excellence, reputation in art might be cheaply earned.   But there go, to make a true architect, far other qualifications than these: original conception, that can shake itself free of previous canons; independent thought; creative genius.   The works of others must be studied, not to believe and repeat, but to probe and anatomize.   There must be sought, not the offspring, but the parent; not the mere superficial details, but the hidden principle that gave birth to them.   If the effect, in any old example, be good, and the combination happy, it should be the effort of the student to catch and master the spirit whence these sprung.   In his hands, perchance, it may produce effects as good, combinations as happy; but stamped with the individuality of his own genius, shaped by the circumstances of country and age and climate, in which he designs, and modified, in each case, by the specific purpose or occasion that may chance to call forth the exercise of his talent.

In recommending, then, the Architecture of the later Norman and earlier Gothic periods, as a promising field of study, I advise no unreserved adoptions, no implicit copyings; no servile reproduction of any one example, in either of the manners; nor even a following out, with chronological fidelity, of the peculiar details that mark any particular era throughout these two centuries.   My advice is but this, that American genius should labor in that prolific field, and exercise a discretion neither tame-spirited nor presumptuous, in selecting and rejecting; in combining old forms and features, and originating new.

There are certain peculiarities which the rude spirit of the age engrafted on this

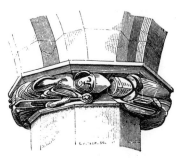

Cottingham, Northants.

Architecture, and which good sense will at once reject. Among these may be reckoned human figures distorted into capitals, as at Cottingham, England; and worse yet, those hideous gurgoyles,* which obtrude their dis-

Gurgoyle,
Horsley Church, Derbyshire.

gusting presence, even in some of the finest specimens of Middle-age Architecture, in strange contrast with the graceful and the picturesque that surround them.   In

---

* It need hardly be said, that everything grotesque has been carefully excluded from the architectural details of the Smithsonian Institution building.   There should be some better reason for imitating the peculiarities of an ancient manner, than that they *are* its peculiarities.

The best and most graceful details for capitals, bosses, the terminating points of brackets, corbel-courses, &c., are supplied by varieties of foliage.

† Spouts connected with gutters, to discharge rain-water; sometimes caricatured human figures; sometimes rude representations of animals, in every attitude of distortion.

Iffley Church,
Oxfordshire.

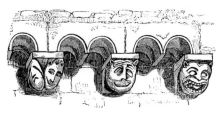

Corbel-course,
Romsey Church, Hants.

the same class of barbarisms are to be included, heads of horrible ugliness, supporting brackets or terminating dripstones, or employed as bosses, or incorporated in mouldings, or repeated in corbel-courses throughout their entire length; and, finally, animals squatted under columns, usually found at the entrance of churches or supporting a pulpit, and supposed to have been originally introduced as a security against evil spirits. Motive and manner, in this last case, are worthy of each other.

Sometimes these aberrations of a vagrant fancy had more of the whimsical about them than of the gravely offensive. An example is shown on the opposite page; a human figure cut in stone, that is made to support the pulpit steps in the Freyberg Cathedral, and to which tradition has attached the story, that it represents a contumacious apprentice, who had incurred the anger, or the envy, of the builder, his master. We smile at the conceit; yet it is not the less to be confessed, that all such vagaries are indefensible; and are to be set down (how variant soever the examples) in the same category as the Caryatides of the Pandrosion, or the giant Atlantes still found among the ruins of Agrigentum.

There are other peculiarities in regard to which difference of opinion may arise; the chief, perhaps, being the form of door and window heads, which some may prefer semicircular, others pointed. I incline to believe, that, for the majority of modern structures, the former will be found the more suitable. We do not commonly require apartments, like the old cathedral nave, of vast height compared to their width; and

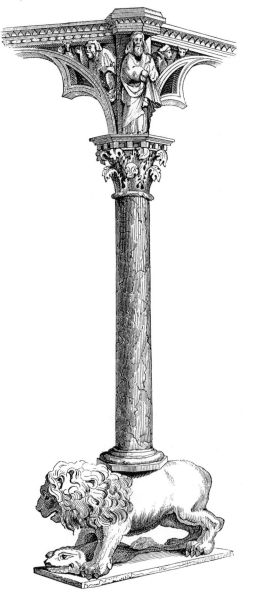

Pulpit, Baptistery of Pisa.

the very pointed roofs that followed pointed arching, and prevailed especially during
the Early English period, are higher and
sharper than are demanded by any snows
on our continent, until we reach the latitude of Canada.

It is an item in favor of the Lombard
variety of Architecture, that it more readily
dispenses with parapets than does the
Gothic. Parapets prevent the roof, no
matter what its pitch, from discarding its
load of snow. In our more northern states,
therefore, it is an advantage to be able to
finish a building front appropriately without
them.

The rounded form of head for doors
and windows, has the advantage of harmonizing better with a flat ceiling, than the
Gothic arch. The former has no pointed
apex, leading the eye upwards; but the
sharp form of the latter seems to suggest,

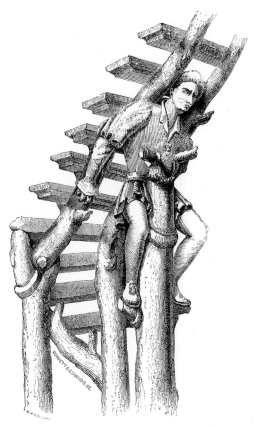

Cathedral of Freyberg, Saxony.*

as conducive to the good keeping of an interior, a vault above.

In the Early English, and more especially in the Lombard style, small pillars, having

Stone Church, Kent.
c. 1280.

bases and capitals, are often employed to divide windows,
or attached to the jambs of windows or of doors. As
a mere subordinate enrichment, I do not conceive that
the same objection holds against these as against the
engaged column of Italian Architecture, of which the
size and classical pretension and ambitious station render it a marked and leading feature, in any elevation in
which it is employed. Yet, as a general rule, the simpler
lines common at a somewhat later date, (sometimes
adopted, too, during the Early English period, and occurring even in some Norman examples,) seem to me
preferable. If a window be divided, it may be done
in a simple and economical manner by the plain mullion, without base or capital to arrest its lines. In the

* There are several European towns of similar name, having Cathedrals that have been figured and

Norman door or window, a simple splay often looks well. Where a little more ornament is desired, jambs with square recesses show to advantage, and there is a good example of a late Norman date, (about 1150,) in which a plain

circular moulding, in the nature of a pillar without base or capital, is continued uninterruptedly, with good effect, up the jambs and around the head of a semicircular headed window.

Cassington, Oxfordshire.
c. 1150.

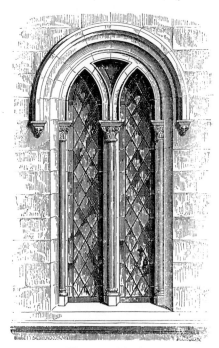

Museum Window,
Smithsonian Institution.

The Gothic window, throughout the greater part of the Early English period, and until near the close of the thirteenth century, is usually found, like the Norman, without a traceried head. Whether the Norman or the Gothic manner be selected, I think window tracery, except of a simple kind, is better omitted. Elaborate tracery is not essential to the grace or finish of an arched construction, unless in the case of an edifice very ambitiously ornamented; and, if it be executed in stone, (as it ought to be, if adopted at all,) it is expensive.

Both Norman and Early English windows are, if we follow the majority of examples, of size and shape not well adapted to modern convenience. The Norman window is commonly too small, and the Early English too narrow. But the former may, without injury to its effect, be enlarged, as has been done throughout the Smithsonian edifice, or divided by a mullion, as in the upper or Museum story of that building; and the latter may be grouped, as in the annexed example, usually with very good effect; nor, if it be desired to avoid

Oundle, Northamptonshire.

described in architectural works; one is Fribourg, in Switzerland, capital of the Canton of the same name. Another, the best known, is Freiburg in Breisgau. Its Cathedral is noted for its open spire, some four hundred and fifteen feet in height, one of the marvels of Continental Architecture.

grouping, is there good reason why it may not be increased, as in some transition examples, to the proportions of the early Decorated.*

The Norman window may also be grouped, as in an example here given from the porch of the east wing of the Smithsonian Institution. The design is simple and good, and might be advantageously copied in Cottage Architecture; to which, it may be said in passing, the Norman manner, in its simplest style, is well adapted.

East Porch,
Smithsonian Institution.

In the interiors of modern churches and lecture-rooms, galleries are frequently introduced; a feature not to be found in the old cathedral.

Caudebec, France.

The innovation within should beget a corresponding change without. It is but a poor expedient, betraying poverty of resource, to suffer the line of a gallery floor to cut across the long side windows, as if it had been an after-thought. The old Freemasons would never have been satisfied with so imperfect an adaptation. Nor should we. Unless a gallery be entirely detached from the walls behind it, and managed so as to appear a mere piece of furniture, the side windows, where the gallery crosses them, ought to be divided into two; the lower having a square head, no matter whether the upper be round or pointed; and the two, perhaps, being in a measure identified as one, by paneling, or some similar expedient. An example, very well managed, occurs in a church at Caudebec, on the Seine, near Rouen.

I shall speak elsewhere of the comparative expense of fire-proofing by iron joists and by groined vaulting. Wherever the latter is preferred, as in public halls of large size I think it usually should be, the buttress naturally and properly follows it. The usual Norman buttress is too flat and pilaster-like in its proportions to afford efficient support, where the lateral thrust is considerable and the intervening wall not massive.

---

* In the later Decorated, in the Perpendicular, and in the Tudor or Elizabethan variety, architects often ran into extravagance, as regards the size of their windows. Of this Bacon complains: "You shall sometimes," says he, "have fair windows so full of glass, that one cannot tell where to come, to be out of the sun."

11

But there is no sufficient reason why the bolder projection, and receding stages, of the Early English buttress should not be introduced among Norman details. A too great depth in buttresses is, indeed, objectionable, especially if the intervals between them be narrow; for, in certain points of view, they confuse the perspective and cover up the windows. An example occurs in an edifice with imposing Norman features, and now in progress of erection in New York; St. George's Church, in Stuyvesant Square.

Pinnacles, scarcely occurring until the thirteenth century, and not abundant throughout the Early English period, should, I think, be sparingly employed (especially in connection with Norman openings) except where their presence is actually demanded by considerations of security, to weight down buttresses; or where these, without such anchorage, must receive, to effect their purpose, unsightly projection. The Early English pinnacle, as in the example from Battle Church, was plain. In late Gothic, niches and canopies formed a portion of its usual ornaments. These should be avoided. Bold carving, however, as the surmounting enrichment of a lofty pinnacle, may often be introduced with excellent effect.

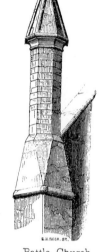

Battle Church,
Sussex.

Under ordinary circumstances, as our public buildings do not usually emulate the cathedral of the Middle Ages in height or architectural daring, the simple buttress, terminating at top either with a plain slope dying into the wall, or with the surmounting finish of a gabled

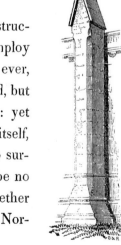

cap, may suffice for all purposes of utility and appearance.

There may seldom, in modern structures, be legitimate occasion to employ the flying buttress; a feature rarely, if ever, introduced during the Norman period, but not uncommon in the Early English: yet whenever occasion fairly presents itself, as, if a vaulted clerestory be made to surmount a lofty building, there should be no scruple in introducing this feature, whether the general style of the building be Norman or Gothic.

Ensham, Oxon.

Whitbey, Yorkshire.

There is, perhaps, no one example in the history of Architecture, in which genius, enlightened by mechanical science and following the lead of utility, more happily united use with ornament, more skillfully availed itself of what seemed an embarrassing necessity, to combine the charm of bold beauty with the attraction of constructive display, than in the instance of this flying buttress. When, for the security of some spacious cathedral, it was first thought essential to set, against the walls of the clerestory (in order to resist and carry off a portion of the side-thrust of its vault) spandrel-shaped props of stone, which, descending to the buttresses of the side-aisles, were, in their turn, braced and sustained by these; the necessity was lamented: and the agent employed was hidden from view, as an unacknowledged expedient, under the side-aisle roof. But, after a time, to some bold thinker it occurred, that what necessity had created, genius might display and taste adorn; and the flying buttress, one of the most striking and effective features in Arch Architecture, was the result. Its history, properly read, conveys a lesson of which the teachings may lead far, and conduct, at last, even to great achievements.*

Buttress under Side-aisle Roof,
Abbaye aux Hommes, (St. Stephen's,) Caen.

* In the case of the flying buttress, as in that of almost all other marked features of Gothic Architecture, the earlier examples are much purer and better than those which occur late in the Florid period. After the victory was fairly achieved, and the flying buttress, emerging from its concealment, stood forth in acknowledged beauty, it gradually reached its most graceful form and obtained its most appropriate enrichment. Thence, with the forms around it, it declined, overloaded with superfluous decoration. If we compare the annexed cut of a flying buttress and pinnacle from Henry VII's Chapel, (A. D. 1510,) with the cut immediately above, giving the same features in an edifice about half a century older, we shall recognize the progress of this degeneracy.

Sherborne, Dorsetshire.

Henry VII's Chapel

The clerestory,* with its high side-lights, is particularly suitable for any large apartment in which the lower walls are to be unbroken by windows and the light is required from above; as in a gallery of art; for which purpose it is employed in the western connecting range of the Smithsonian building.

In interiors, whether the semicircular or the pointed arch be employed, I think unity and propriety are best consulted by wholly discarding the single, round column, even though deprived of all classical proportion and resemblance. It is, indeed, common in Norman Architecture to adopt a plain column, from the capital of which, as an impost, ribs for groining spring. But to this the objections have already been stated. And if, in addition, fancy be allowed a voice in such matters, the *faisceau*, the bundle of reeds deriving their strength from their union, seems more appropriate in American Architecture, than the single consolidated column, standing alone and apart, in solitary grandeur.

In some early Gothic pillars, those of Westminster Abbey for instance, horizontal

Westminster Abbey.

bands are introduced, at intervals, across the shaft. A modern example may be seen in the interior of the Church of the Divine Unity, (Mr. Bellows',) in Broadway, New York. It is evidently a blemish, to be avoided; a violation of the vertical principle, trifling, indeed, in character, but still without necessity or excuse.

As regards the vertical principle generally, I think it greatly conducive to unity and purity of style that it should be allowed to govern in Arch Architecture, to the full extent which the nature of the case may permit. We ought not, indeed, to wander off from utility, in search of undue elevation, for the mere sake of more closely applying that or any other elementary rule. And, in a general way, we cannot

* That upper portion of the middle aisle of a Norman or Gothic cathedral which shows above its side-aisles, and has a tier or row of windows on each side looking clear over the side-aisle roof, is called the *clerestory*, or *clearstory*. The interior walls of the side-aisles, continued upwards, become the exterior walls of the clerestory. It was probably adopted at first as a means of giving increased light in the body of the cathedral; of which the only side-lights, must, but for this expedient, have come from the low and distant side-aisle windows. Its external appearance may be judged by inspecting the plate of the exterior of Grace Church; and, on a small

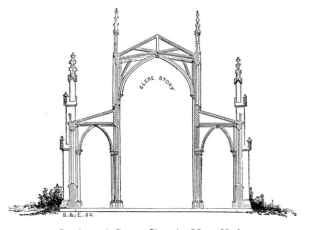

Section of Grace Church, New York.

expect, in buildings erected to suit modern convenience, that loftiness, of which the architects of the Middle Ages so happily availed themselves, in this connection. Yet we may do well enough, if we but make the most of our opportunities. We often fail, not because the limits within which we labor are hopelessly circumscribed, but because we neglect the means, strictly within our reach, of advancement and success.

An architect who works in the Norman manner ought to be specially on his guard against the cutting up of vertical lines; since most of the examples he is likely to study are more or less faulty in that respect. The Smithsonian design is, I think, more free from that defect than any ancient building with which I am acquainted, that is known to date strictly within the Norman era.

If, on the other hand, he select his starting-point from among Gothic models, then he ought carefully to avoid multiplicity of detail and profusion of ornament; errors into which, after studying the Pointed Style, especially in its later phases, there is constant temptation to run. We ought to bear in mind, that rich and multiform decorations, which, on a grand scale, become imposing and rise to magnificence, may degenerate into whim and tinsel, when mimicked in a petty way, and shorn of the effect which was due, in a measure, to their magnitude.

If an architect be gifted with a moderate degree of resource, he will find little difficulty in adapting Arch Architecture, without sacrifice of effect, to the varying wants and purposes, which his designs may be required to clothe. He may, in every case, begin, as a good designer always will, from within; and, let the character of the edifice be what it will, ecclesiastical, legislative, executive, commercial or collegiate, he may find, among the thousand expressions which its changeful aspects assume, one that shall be appropriate.

The ground-plan of the Smithsonian edifice was, in substance, determined, before even the style of Architecture was fixed upon, in which its various interiors were to be invested. Yet I do not think it wanting in harmony or general effect; nor do I believe that any one, of moderately cultivated taste, in looking upon that building, would mistake its character, or connect it, in his mind, with other than a scientific or collegiate foundation.

Its two wings, also, seem to me intelligibly stamped with the general character of object, for which they are, respectively, designed: the east wing, next to the Capitol,

scale, it is shown in the perspective view of the west wing of the Smithsonian Institution, both plates given in a previous portion of this chapter. In the latter the small clerestory windows of the Gallery of Art may be seen, on the left of the cut, above, and back of, the open arches of the cloister.

The clerestory is a very economical method of obtaining elevation for an upper hall: the whole of what would otherwise be garret becoming available. An example is found in the New York Free Academy, figured in Chapter VIII.

set apart for the severer sciences, as Chemistry and Natural Philosophy, hinting, by its solid and somewhat massive outline, at gravity of purpose; while the west wing, intended to contain a Gallery of Art, intimates, by its lighter proportions and airier forms, the spirit, more of grace and ornament, of its destination. Convenience should never be sacrificed thus to obtain a result, which many will pronounce fanciful. Yet where the poetry of Architecture can be introduced without injury to the prose of practical adaptation, true genius will not reject its aid.

In connection with the foregoing pages, having for object to aid, in as far as a few brief hints may, the advancement of a useful and a liberal art, and as well to stir up in American architects a desire to become more than copyists—an ambition gradually to work out and establish a manner that may be claimed as their own—as also to indicate to the student a promising direction for the labors tending to such an object; it may be useful to devote a short chapter more specially to the inquiry, how far, in such a pursuit, we may wisely follow the lead of custom, and when we may profitably deviate from the beaten track.

Netley Abbey, Hampshire.

CHAPTER VII.

OF ANACHRONISMS IN ARCHITECTURE.

"We ought to have sense and taste enough not to burden ourselves, in the pursuit of beauty, with shackles of our own creating."

HOPE'S HISTORICAL ESSAY.

THE geologist does not classify and arrange, with more critical accuracy, those fossil relics that mark the ages of various formations, nor more carefully subdivide these into genera and species, than do some architects, smitten with antiquarian scruple, lay down the boundaries, and disinter the inorganic remains, and classify the slightest peculiarities of form or modifications of ornament, that serve to determine the successive styles of Architecture, as these prevailed throughout different ages of the world. And this palæontology of Architecture is not without its interest or its use, both as a merely speculative and curious branch of research, and as an instructive preliminary investigation for the professional student.

But when the antiquary becomes the lawgiver; when that which has been, is made the despotic precedent for that which is to be; when it is declared to the modern architect, that, if he adopt the leading features of some ancient manner, he shall confine himself also, with religious strictness and even in the simplest form or minutest ornament, to precedents out of the style he may have selected, and to which, as to a bill of rights, he can alone refer, if his authority be brought into question; then the knowledge which should serve to guide and to assist, may be perverted so as only to clog and to hinder.

It is very true, also, that the spirit of innovation may be pushed beyond reasonable limit. To the creating and combining into a distinctive whole of any style of Architure that may aspire to the dignity of a separate school, there must have gone much careful thought. The genius of many successive artists must have been bent to mould gracefully its forms, to harmonize its separate members, to perfect its details. And to such considerations, before we depart from the precedents thus set, due weight should be given. When we leave the beaten track, it is much easier to introduce incongruities than improvements. That is no good reason why we should *not* leave it; but it is a very good and sufficient one, why, in so doing, we should jealously examine, in all its aspects and relations, any innovation we may be tempted to adopt.

Nor do I consider it valid cause, or sufficient apology, for innovation, that there is no good reason against it. If there be not good reason *for* it, it will be set down, in the minds of men, as idle caprice or willful heresy. There is a certain violence done to the feelings of the mass of mankind, when old and venerated associations are broken up; when the ancient landmark is removed. On the one hand, we should not do this, for light cause; on the other, when there is cause sufficient, we should not scruple to do it.

One of the commentators on Vitruvius, speaking of the mixing of different Grecian orders, says: " This incongruity, although invariably revolting to the eye of taste, is, in fact, perhaps, only apparent; for there is nothing in the members themselves, which, when joined, should render them unfit for the purposes of strength and utility; but from the long observation of a contrary practice, recommended by so many powerful associations, we have become impressed with that idea, which it is now impossible to eradicate."*

If some architect, without adequate and apparent cause to show for his latitudinari-anism, were to transpose the members that now distinguish and determine the separate orders;—imposing, perhaps, on the Doric frieze, with its triglyphs and its metopes, the Ionic cornice; or surmounting the rich capital of the Corinthians with the heavy entablature of Tuscany;—such aberration from ancient usage would strike men's minds as a capricious affectation, or an unprovoked offence. Nonconformity invites attack; and should, therefore, be well provided with defence.

Nor is it probable, that good and sufficient reason could be given, for any such change. The Greeks had a quick and cultivated perception of fitness and grace; and in the peculiar manner to which they were restricted, it would be difficult to correct, or surpass them.

But in Architecture, as in every other department of human knowledge, there is an element of progress. And Architecture, too, has its blind conservatism, allied to bigotry. In Architecture, as in law, what to-day is fact, to-morrow becomes doctrine. The architect who innovates, no matter how happily, is cried down, by the orthodox of his profession, as an ignorant blunderer or a graceless heretic.

To this wholesale persecution—this indiscriminate condemnation without a hear-ing—of whatever is new and unconforming, I object. It is contrary to the spirit of our age. It is foreign to the genius of our country. America disdains not to learn from other nations: but her ambition rises higher than merely to imitate; she seeks to go beyond them.

If, as has been recommended in a previous chapter, some variety of the later Nor-

* Wilkins' *Introduction to Vitruvius*, p. 9.

man or early Gothic should be selected, as a stock whereupon to graft a national style of Architecture for these States, the latitude for which I have here been pleading, prudently exercised, will prove highly advantageous. It will suffer us to combine the more finished construction and more graceful forms of a later era with the imposing simplicity of an earlier one. It will enable us to avoid, alike, the clumsiness and lingering incongruities of one period, and the profuse decoration and overloaded ornament of another.

I do not think it essential, though many architects do, that the mouldings, mullions, capitals, corbel-courses, window tracery, (if it be employed,) buttresses, pinnacles, and other details belonging to one particular era of Arch Architecture, should be peremptorily excluded from every other.* Between many of the details that are peculiar

* The superficial critic often condemns, as an anachronism, what, in truth, is none. I have heard it more than once remarked, that the *quatre-foil*, freely used in the Smithsonian building, was not to be found in any ancient example of the Norman or Lombard style. This is not so. Cotman, in his "Architectural Antiquities of Normandy," says:

Quatre-foil,
Hargrave, Northamptonshire.

"Taken as a whole, the church of Bieville has, probably, no parallel in Normandy or in England. The upper story of the tower alone is of a subsequent era, and that, the earliest style of Pointed Architecture. All the rest of the structure *is purely Norman*, and of extreme simplicity." * * "The basement contains only the door, which is entered by a richly ornamented arch, surmounted by a broad dripstone, *decorated with quatre-foils.*"

This door is figured in Plate 59 of Cotman's work.

In the Abbey Church of St. Stephen's (L'Abbaye aux Hommes) at Caen, described both by Pugin and Cotman, and by the former expressly declared to afford "a specimen of genuine Norman Architecture," occurs a balustrade of open quatre-foils; and though Pugin speaks of it as "apparently of modern introduction," Cotman dissents from that opinion. He says:

Church of the Holy Trinity, Caen.

"Immediately upon entering the church, a doubt involuntarily suggests itself, how far this balustrade may not be an addition of comparatively modern date. But, upon the whole, there seems no reason to consider it so. Precisely the same ornament is found on the tomb of Berengaria, wife to Richard Cœur de Lion, which Mr. Stothard has lately figured, and believes to be coeval with the queen it commemorates."—*Cotman's Normandy*, vol. i, p. 25.

So, also, in another Caen Church, (that of the Holy Trinity, A. D. 1066 to 1082,) of which Cotman says, "A more perfect specimen of a Norman abbatial church is nowhere to be found," the east end of the choir forming a circular apse, has a similar ornament. That author remarks:

"The balustrade of open quatre-foils above, appears coeval with the rest, and may be regarded as tending to establish the originality of that in the nave of St. Stephen."—*Cotman*, vol. i, p. 32.

These examples Pugin must have overlooked, when he says:

"A line of quatre-foils may be seen at the Church of St. Giles', at Evreux. This ornament, so exceed-

to different eras of that changeful and diversified manner, there is no natural and inherent incongruity, but a mere conventional one, which it requires antiquarian acumen to detect and expose. And the true principle is, that laws of mere convention may properly be set aside, at the bidding of taste or of utility. It should go for nothing, merely to convict an architect of anachronism in his details; such license may be not only innocent but commendable.

The capitals peculiar to the Early English style of Gothic seem to me, in a general way, more graceful than the Norman. If, then, I were designing an edifice with circular-headed openings, I should not scruple to employ the former, though there be no old example of circular or octagonal capitals in this latter connection. And for this my sufficient reason would be, that I hold the prevalence of square projections and rectangular faces, running through the early Norman, to be essentially a blemish, injurious to the effect of that style. So, also, in a Lombard building, if constructive convenience demanded it, I would not hesitate to give to the buttress a size and form, for which

Stone Church, Kent.

precedent can be found in Gothic eras only. And if, in such a case, I perceived, that to afford complete security to the building its buttresses were about to assume an inconvenient or unsightly depth, I would not be deterred from taking some simple form of pinnacle as a remedy, by the mere fact, that pinnacles were an expedient not adopted until after the Norman arch had fallen into disuse. Pinnacles, if not elaborately enriched, harmonize well with the Norman manner; and, in truth, their anchoring aid is more likely to be required in connection with the lower arch of that style than with the higher and sharper Gothic; since the higher the arch, the less in proportion, all other things being equal, is its lateral pressure.

On the other hand, if there were question of mixing, in the same elevation, Norman and Gothic windows, though the utility of the building would not thereby be injured, and though, in numerous transition examples, there be old precedent for it, such incongruity would seem to me an offence—not certainly a grievous one, but an offence still—against unity and harmony of design; and, as such, a blemish that

ingly common in the Pointed Style, is said to be met in this one Norman building only."—*Introd. to Antiqu. of Caen*, p. 12.

It is evident, then, that the quatre-foil has occasionally been used in the semicircular style. But even if it had not, I should not scruple to introduce it from a somewhat later era, as an ornament graceful in itself, and appropriate to the Norman manner.

should be avoided.   There can be no motive, save a purely fanciful one, for indulging in such an aberration.

Again: such an anachronism as rich Gothic tracery in a Norman window is little defensible.   One of the recommendations of the Norman style is its graceful simplicity; and we ought not to risk injury to that effect by interpolating, from another manner, an enrichment unnecessary and expensive.

Without running into further details, which will readily suggest themselves to any well-informed architectural student, let it suffice to assert the principle, that an anachronism in Architecture may be either a merit, a whim, or an offence: a merit, when the foreign feature introduced is demanded by utility, harmonizes with the spirit of the style upon which it is engrafted, adds a new beauty or corrects an old defect; a whim, when the innovation is a mere fanciful variety, adding nothing of useful, or graceful, or appropriate, beyond what the original details of the style sufficed to supply; and an offence, when the exotic is transplanted into a soil unsuited to its growth; when the anachronism produces incongruity, not conventional merely, but natural and inherent.

To the genius of the architect it must, in each case, be left, to determine the exact line of demarcation, between intemperate license and barren servility.

Decorated Window Tracery,
South Dutch Church, New York.

CHAPTER VIII.

SOME ITEMS INDICATING THE COMPARATIVE COST OF THE ARCH AND OF THE POST AND LINTEL MANNERS.

In deciding the relative merits of different manners of Architecture, each carried out faithfully in its appropriate style and material, the item of their comparative cost must ever remain an important one.

I purpose here to furnish a few data, which, though insufficient in themselves to settle the questions that arise in this connection, may yet assist in enabling Building Committees, and other public bodies charged with important constructions, to form some judgment in the premises.

There are four large public buildings at our Seat of Government; all columnar structures; or, in other words, all exhibiting the exterior forms of the Post and Lintel manner: one a Roman building, the Capitol; two others adorned with Grecian colonnade and portico, namely, the Treasury Building and the Patent Office; and one in the modern Italian or Palladian style, the Post Office. Their cost and dimensions, estimated in cubical feet of contents, are as follows:

The Capitol, four stories in height, and of which the main building has a front of 352 feet, cost, including the expense of rebuilding after its partial destruction in 1814, and the laying out of its grounds, $2,659,573. The building, making a fair allowance for these incidental expenses not properly entering into its cost, may be estimated to have cost somewhere between two millions and two millions and a quarter. Its cubical contents are 4,147,400 feet. It has cost, therefore, fully *fifty cents* per cubic foot.

The Treasury Building, with four stories, a length of 336 feet and an Ionic colonnade and portico of 37 columns, cost $648,743. Its cubical contents are 1,944,740 feet. It has cost, therefore, about *thirty-three and one-third cents* per cubic foot.

The Patent Office, with three floors, has a front of 270 feet, from the centre of which projects a Doric portico of sixteen columns. Its cubical contents are 1,466,660 feet; and its cost was $417,550; or nearly *thirty cents* per cubic foot.*

* The cost of these buildings is taken from *House Doc. Rep. No.* 267, 28*th Cong.*, 1*st Sess.* The cubical contents of each building have been supplied to me by Mr. Robert Mills, formerly public architect, and who furnished the plans for the Treasury Building and Post Office.

In estimating the cubical contents, the entire area is multiplied by the height, without any deduction for walls; and the basement, but not the garret, and the colonnade, or portico, where these occur, are included.

On Stone by C.W.Burton.

Renwick Archt.

GRACE CHURCH from Broadway NEW YORK.

Ackermans lith. 120 Fulton St N.Y.

These buildings are all erected of a sandstone of faulty character, with many blemishes and iron stains, derived from the, quarries of Acquia Creek, Virginia, near the Potomac, some fifty miles below Washington.*   The average cost of this material was not less than *forty-five cents* per cubic foot of dimension stone, delivered in Washington; more than double the cost of that employed in the Smithsonian building. It has been covered up in the Capitol by several coats of paint, laid on over the entire exterior of that building; and which give to it, at a distance, the appearance of a marble structure.

The General Post Office, four stories high, of marble from New York, and adorned with engaged columns and pilasters, having Corinthian capitals, was erected, by contract, at a cost of $452,765.   Its cubical contents are 1,071,252 feet.   Its cost, per cubic foot, was, therefore, about *forty-two and a half cents.*

In comparing, however, the cost of these three last-mentioned buildings, in justice to the Palladian style it should be remembered, that the whole of the cubical contents of the Post Office are distributed over rooms or passages essentially useful, whereas the colonnade and portico of the Treasury Building, containing 416,880 cubic feet, and the portico of the Patent Office, containing 212,160 cubic feet, must be regarded as ornamental features, not available for business purposes.   Deducting these, and estimating the interior available space only, the cost of the Treasury Building, for each cubic foot, rises to about *forty-two and a half cents*, and of the Patent Office to *thirty-three and a third cents.*

Of two other important public buildings recently erected by the General Government, the general character, cost and cubical contents are as follows :†

The New York Custom-house is after the temple model, of marble, with a portico and posticum, each of eight fluted Doric columns, and has deep pilasters along its flanks.   The dome over its principal business-room does not show externally.   The building has four stories.   Its cubical contents (including its porticoes) being about 906,000 feet, and its cost $960,000; the result is nearly *one dollar and six cents* per cubic foot.

The Boston Custom-house, of granite, is a parallelogram, 140 feet by 76, with a Doric portico of six fluted pillars, projecting in the centre of each of its long sides. It is surmounted by a dome, covered in with granite slabs, the only example of the kind, so far as I know, in the world.   Between the windows around the whole building, so far as it is not covered by its porticoes, are columns attached to the wall.   Its

* For particulars regarding this building material, unfit for use where permanence and durability are required, see Appendix, Note A.

† These particulars have been furnished, for the present work, from the Treasury Department of the United States.

cubical contents, including its porticoes and dome, are about 730,000 feet, and its cost $776,000,* or upwards of *one dollar and six cents* per cubic foot.

Two other Grecian structures, of imposing exterior, the one in the occupation of the United States, and the other devoted to the purposes of a private charity, deserve notice.

The building originally erected for the Bank of the United States, in Chestnut street, Philadelphia, since sold to the United States, and now occupied as a Custom-house, is in the temple form, of marble, with a portico and posticum, each of eight Doric columns, without bases. It has neither columns nor pilasters on the flanks. Its cubical contents, including its porticoes, are 530,613 feet; and its cost was $257,452; that is, about *forty-eight cents and a half* per cubic foot.

The Girard College, including the area of its peristyle, to the edge of its outer steps, stands on 34,344 superficial feet; or, excluding the peristyle, on 18,759. The average height of the cella, including its three stories and its basement, is about 90 feet; of the peristyle, 55 feet. The cubical contents, then, including the peristyle, are 2,545,485 feet. Its cost, as furnished to me by its architect, was about $1,427,800 ;† or upwards of *fifty-six cents* per cubic foot.

All these buildings are rendered fire-proof by vaulting, chiefly by groined vaulting; yet none of them have the exterior appropriate to arched construction.‡

The porticoes of the New York and Philadelphia and Boston Custom-houses, the dome of the latter and the colonnade of the Girard College, though doubtless of occasional utility, cannot fairly be regarded as furnishing necessary or available space for business or collegiate purposes. The cubical contents of the portico and posticum of the New York Custom-house are about 147,000 feet, and of the Philadelphia Cus-

---

* This does not include the price of lot, nor the very heavy cost incurred in preparing for the stone foundations ; these two items amounting to about $300,000; and making the total cost of this Custom-house, including lot and foundations, $1,076,000. The two porticoes and dome cost, according to the statement of the architect, $240,000.

The cost of this building was increased by the large size of the blocks employed in its construction, and by the high finish given to much of its granite work.

† The entire cost of the Girard buildings, including enclosure, &c. was $1,933,821. Of this, the eastern and western outbuildings cost nearly $414,000; the enclosure, about $65,000; the farm-house, $8,500; and other incidentals, between $19,000 and $20,000 : making about $507,000 to be deducted from the total of $1,933,821, to give the cost of the College building, as above stated.

‡ The necessity for the buttress, in vaulted structures, is less strict, when the rooms vaulted, as often occurs in these buildings, are of small size. Yet, in the New York Custom-house, as in a description furnished to me by its architect, we learn, it was thought necessary to resort, as in the Girard College, to iron banding. The words are : " Every point of lateral thrust from the arches or other pressure is guarded and held secure by the strong arm of iron. Chainings made of bars four inches broad and one inch in thickness, and of the best quality of wrought iron, extend across the building in every direction."—*New York Commercial Advertiser of July* 13, 1842.

tom-house about 52,200 feet; that of the porticoes and dome of the Boston Custom-house, about 110,000 feet; and of the peristyle of the Girard College 857,175 feet. If, then, as in the case of the Washington buildings, we estimate the cubical contents of the *available* interiors only, the cost will rise, in the New York Custom-house, to upwards of *one dollar and twenty-six cents;* in the Philadelphia Custom-house to upwards of *fifty-three cents and three-quarters;* in the Boston Custom-house to about *one dollar and twenty-five cents;* and, in the Girard College, to about *eighty-four and a half cents,* for each cubic foot.

We have, unfortunately, no erections clothed with the appropriate exteriors of Arch Architecture, which may be strictly compared, as to cost, with the Grecian and Roman buildings here estimated. Almost all the public buildings in our country, which are executed, in creditable style, in the Gothic manner, are ecclesiastical; their internal plan, of course, being entirely different from that of edifices erected for commercial or executive or collegiate purposes; since they are usually finished with lofty spires, and, in the body of the building, without partition walls subdividing them into small apartments. And few, if any of these, are absolutely fire-proof, or fully possess that character of solidity and permanence which appertains to the Girard College and to some of the government buildings above referred to, especially the Custom-houses of which the cost has been given. Of public buildings in the Norman style, except two or three churches in and near New York, the Smithsonian building is the only appropriate example.

The materials for comparison, then, are scanty, and most of the results they furnish must be received as an approximation only to a strictly accurate result. Still, estimates of a few Gothic and Norman structures may supply data of some value, in making out a comparison between the cost of the Arch and the Post and Lintel manners, respectively.

Trinity Church, at the head of Wall street, New York, is an edifice in the Perpendicular Gothic style, and after the old cathedral model, but without a transept, very substantially and handsomely built, of freestone from the New Red Sandstone formation, similar in quality to that employed in the Smithsonian building, and with a stone spire two hundred and eighty-four feet high. Its cubical contents, including its vestry and its tower, to the base of the pyramidal spire, (but excluding the contents of the spire, as not of strict use or available,) are 821,070 cubic feet. It has cost about $338,000; of which about one-third was expended on its tower and spire. Its cost, per cubic foot, is, therefore, upwards of *forty-one cents.* The cubical contents of its tower are 159,250 feet. If it had been finished without tower or spire, it would have cost about *thirty-four cents* per cubic foot.

Grace Church, in Broadway, New York, is a sparkling specimen, on a small scale, of a cathedral, with transept, in the style of Gothic prevailing on the European Continent about the commencement of the fifteenth century, the early Flamboyant.* It is of marble, from the quarries of Sing Sing, except its pyramidal spire, reaching an elevation of two hundred and forty feet, which is finished, as in some old examples, of wood. Its cubical contents, including its square tower to the base of the spire, are 505,230 cubic feet, and its cost was about $80,000; of which about $17,000 was expended on its tower and spire. Its cost is, therefore, nearly *sixteen cents* per cubic foot. The cubical contents of its tower being 75,816 feet, it would have cost, without tower or spire, about *fourteen and two-third cents* per cubic foot.

The Church of the Puritans, in Union Square, New York, is an example, without much embellishing ornament, of the later Norman or Lombard. It is of marble; one side and the rear of the church, however, being of brick, plastered. The entrance is between two towers, of unequal heights, of which the higher, yet unfinished, is 104 feet in height. It has no spire. Its cubical contents, including its towers, are 540,000 feet; and its cost was $40,000; making nearly *seven and a half cents* per cubic foot.

In both of these last-named churches the interiors, including the pillars and their capitals, are finished with plaster. In Trinity Church the pillars and capitals are of cut stone; and the interior is plastered only above the spring of the side-aisle arches.

The building now in progress of erection for the Smithsonian Institution, and of which a detailed description is given in the next chapter, furnishes a more appropriate subject for comparison as to cost with the public buildings first mentioned, than any edifice arranged as a church or cathedral can. Like a Custom-house or a building for executive purposes, it is subdivided into numerous rooms and halls; and its central portion has two stories, besides its basement.

Its cost, when completed, may be set down at $215,000;† and its cubical contents, including its towers, are 1,545,000 feet. The whole of this space may be regarded as strictly useful,‡ except that upper portion of its towers, which does not afford available rooms, containing 22,000 cubic feet. Deducting this, we have 1,523,000 cubic feet of available contents; at a cost of upwards of *fourteen cents* per cubic foot.

---

* A plate representing Grace Church faces the commencement of this chapter.

† The contract price for the Smithsonian building, completed, is $205,250. But this includes fittings and furniture, estimated at $10,000; leaving the actual contract price for the building at $195,250. To this is to be added, for architect's and superintendent's salaries, and incidentals connected with superintendence until the final completion of the building, $16,000; making, in all, $211,260. There have, however, up to the present time, (when somewhat more than a third of the building is completed,) been additions made to the original contract, to the amount of $680. If we suppose the additions which may be made, during the remainder of the contract, to run up to about $3,000 more; then we have a total of $215,000, as above given. The Building Committee entertain entire confidence, that the contractor, unless prevented by accident not to be foreseen or anticipated, will complete the work at contract prices.

‡ The cloisters are essential, as the only direct passages of communication between the wings and the main building.

It is to be borne in mind, however, as in the next chapter stated, that a portion only of this building is thoroughly fire-proofed. To have made the whole building as completely fire-proof as the Girard College, or the New York and Boston Custom-houses, would have cost, according to a careful estimate made by the architect, *forty-eight thousand dollars*, in addition to the present contract price. The entire cost of the building, therefore, if rendered thoroughly fire-proof, would have amounted to $263,000; or about *seventeen and a quarter cents* per cubic foot.

There is another building, of academical character and in the Gothic style, recently erected by the City Corporation of New York, which merits notice here, on account of its small cost as compared to its appearance and the accommodations it affords. It is the Free Academy, on Lexington Avenue, near Twenty-third street; built of brick,

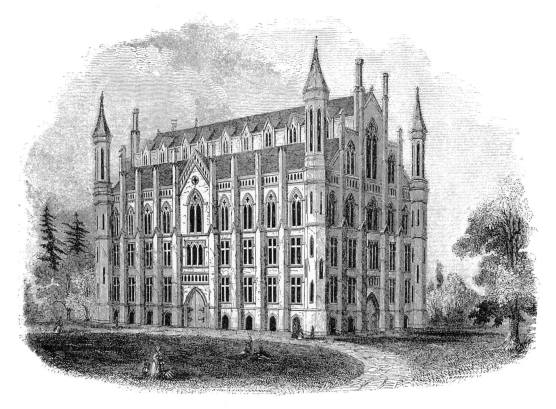

Free Academy, New York.

in compact form, five stories high, including its basement and clerestory. Its cubical contents, all available, are 814,300 feet; and its cost was $48,000; making less than *six cents* per cubic foot.

This building is not fire-proofed. To have made it thoroughly so would have required, according to the estimate of its architect, nearly fifty per cent. addition to its actual cost; which, in that case, would have risen to nearly *nine cents* per foot of cubical contents.

Excluding from comparison the churches, for reasons above given, and estimating the two last buildings at their cost, if thoroughly fire-proofed, we have the results of the foregoing estimates condensed in the following

TABLE OF COMPARATIVE COST OF VARIOUS PUBLIC BUILDINGS.

NAME.	LOCATION.	MATERIAL.	STYLE.	COST PER CUBIC FOOT OF AVAILABLE CONTENTS.
Treasury Building, - -	Washington.	Acquia Creek Freestone.	Grecian, with colonnade.	42½ cents.
United States Patent Office,	Do.	Do. do.	Do. with portico.	33⅓ "
General Post Office, - -	Do.	Marble.	Italian or Palladian.	42½ "
Custom-house, - - - -	New York.	Marble.	Grecian, with porticoes.	126 "
Custom-house, - - - -	Philadelphia.	Marble.	Do. do.	53¾ "
Custom-house, - - - -	Boston.	Granite.	Roman, with dome and porticoes.	125 "
Girard College for Orphans,	Philadelphia.	Marble.	Grecian, with peristyle.	84½ "
Smithsonian Institution, -	Washington.	Seneca Creek Freestone.	Norman, with towers.	17¼ "
Free Academy, - - -	New York.	Brick.	Gothic, with clerestory.	9 "

The results here exhibited, are, it will be confessed, of a striking character, and well worthy to arrest public attention. An inspection of the views and plans given among the illustrations of this volume must satisfy every one, that, in the case of the Smithsonian building, reasonable attention has been given to architectural manner and external embellishment. Nor, as the cut of the Free Academy given on a preceding page may witness, is the style of that building bald or unpleasing. Yet the Smithsonian Institution, if completely fire-proofed, would have cost, (estimating available contents,) but about *one-half* as much as the cheapest of the above public buildings in Washington; less than *one-third* as much as the former United States Bank in Philadelphia ; about *one-fifth* as much as the Girard College ; and less than *one-seventh* of what the New York and Boston Custom-houses have cost the General Government. The cost of the Girard College peristyle alone would have sufficed to erect two Smithsonian Institutions, and have left a hundred and sixty-seven thousand dollars to spare.* In like manner, without multiplying calculations which each can make for himself, every cubic foot available in the Free Academy has cost the City of New York *less than one-twentieth* of what the same space has cost the United States in the Custom-house of that city; and if the Academy had been fire-proofed, it would still have been obtained at *one-fourteenth part* of the cost, as compared with the Government building.

It is to be regretted that the materials for this comparison are not more full and decisive. Yet a mere glance at the above results will leave it no longer matter of doubt, that public buildings, reputable and pleasing in appearance, and in every way suitable for the purposes to which they are devoted, may be erected at a much smaller cost than is usually incurred, especially by the General Government in its erections.

* See page 39.

James Renwick Jr. Architect.

on Stone by [illegible]

GOTHIC DESIGN FOR SMITHSONIAN INSTITUTION.

It must be recollected, however, that many incidental items may considerably vary this cost. If marble be selected as a material, it will, in most situations, make a difference of from *two* to *three cents* per foot of cubical contents, over freestone. I consider marble of ordinary quality, as the large-crystalled marble of Maryland, scarcely superior, either for permanence or appearance, in Gothic or Norman buildings, to a good-tinted and durable freestone, say from the New Red Sandstone formation; such, for example, as the lilac grey variety, used for the Smithsonian building.

But when the pure Grecian manner, or the Roman or Italian style, is adopted, marble is doubtless more appropriate and beautiful than any freestone, be its tint or quality what it will. In estimating the relative cost of the Arch manner, as compared with that of the Post and Lintel, appropriately carried out, this is no inconsiderable item.

Again, the exact cost of a building depends, to some extent, upon the chance of arranging its apartments in a compact form. The same cubical dimensions as those of the Smithsonian building might have been obtained at less cost, had it been possible, with due regard to light, safety and convenience, to throw its various rooms and halls into one large central building, several stories in height; its ground-plan a simple parallelogram, or perhaps approaching a square; and thus dispense with its wings and connecting ranges.* To obtain a chemical department apart from the main building, and a Gallery of Art lighted from above, some additional expense was incurred.

In some peculiar situations, also, as in that of the Boston Custom-house, which rests on piles, considerable additional cost is necessary to procure a reliable foundation.

Again, the cost per cubic foot of interior dimensions in any public building must, in a measure, depend upon the number of compartments into which any given space is required to be subdivided; usually increasing in proportion to that number.

Under ordinary circumstances, however, and where durable material can be procured with reasonable facility, it is my opinion that a public building, for purposes of legislation, justice, commerce, or for ecclesiastical or collegiate purposes, fire-proof, of solid and permanent construction, and of creditable and graceful exterior, may be completed at a cost not exceeding from *twenty* to *twenty-five cents* per cubic foot.†

If this be so: if for twenty cents, or (to leave a margin for contingent sources of extra cost) if for TWENTY-FIVE CENTS per cubic foot of interior contents, public buildings can be erected, not merely substantial or durable, but of handsome and pleasing form and finish; is it just or proper, nay, is it honest or justifiable in any sense, that,

---

* See note to page 104, in connection with plate facing this page.

† The cubical contents of a building are here supposed to be estimated, as in the previous examples, for the sake of simplifying the calculation, they have been: that is to say, by multiplying the area on which the building stands by its height from the floor of the basement to the ceiling of the upper story, without any deduction, either for outer or partition walls or for intervening floors.

out of public funds derived from taxation, or out of the endowments of private benevolence consecrated to human improvement, twice, thrice, yes, more than five times that cost should be lavished to emulate the sumptuous magnificence of ages and of nations that have long since passed away?

To an item of some importance connected with the cost of fire-proof buildings, it may be useful here briefly to advert. It is the relative expense of the two different modes of fire-proofing; to wit, by iron joists and girders, and by brick vaulting.

If we assume the price of iron joists to be two and a half cents a pound; of brick· laid to be twelve dollars per thousand, and of spandrel backing to be thirteen cents per cubic foot; basing our calculations upon the experiments and formulæ of Mr. Hodgkinson, to whom we are indebted for the best experiments extant on the strength of cast iron; we obtain the following results, as to the cost of room-floors or ceilings constructed with cast-iron beams having brick arches thrown between them, when compared with their cost if brick groined arches be substituted.

For a room eighteen feet square, the iron beams with arches would cost	$135
And the brick groined arches would cost - - - -	115
Making the groined arching cheaper, by - - - -	$20
For a room twenty-four feet square the iron beam with arches would cost	$310
And the brick groined arches would cost - - - -	330
Making the iron joists cheaper, by - - - - -	$20

In a room of thirty-six feet square, the difference is still greater in favor of iron beams, being about forty-five dollars; and the difference increases as the size of the room is increased.

These calculations are based on the supposition that the walls, in both instances, are of equal thickness, and the lateral thrust taken off by wrought-iron ties.

It will be perceived, then, that in the floors and ceilings of ordinary-sized rooms, there is but little difference in the cost of these two modes of fire-proofing. But there are other considerations, apart from mere economy of construction, which properly determine the choice between the two methods.

In all buildings where economy of space is required, such as storehouses, manufactories, and dwellings, iron beams have this advantage over brick arching, that they take up but little more space than wooden girders, and therefore afford greater room for storage or for the reception of machinery. In great spans, it is an economical arrangement, to support them by cast-iron columns.

On the other hand, in the ceilings of legislative chambers, of churches and of public halls generally, the groined arch, while its superior beauty will not be denied, will usually be found, under a proper plan of construction, as economical as the iron beam.   For in this case, instead of the massive arches, required, in manufactories for example, to sustain ponderous machinery, the vault may be light, having nothing to support but the roof of the structure.

It may be remarked, in this connection, that the ribs with deep mouldings intersecting each other on the Norman or Gothic vault, and thus panelling its surface, are not to be taken as mere ornamental features.   In churches or halls designed for public speaking, as also in spacious school-rooms or the like, if the ceiling, whether flat or arched, be deeply panelled, the reverberation of the voice is checked, so as greatly to aid the speaker.*   Had the caissons in the dome over the Representatives' Hall in the Capitol been actually sunk, as in that over the Senate Chamber, instead of being merely painted on a smooth surface, it would undoubtedly have rendered that Chamber somewhat more suitable for public speaking.

When iron joists bearing brick arches are employed, the ceiling of a public room may be finished, at small cost, in accordance with the above principle.   A vertical section showing a portion of the ceiling, which presents a succession of low, barrel arches, will readily suggest the manner of doing this.   By covering the projecting lines of joists with deep

Section of Ceiling exposed.

mouldings and plastering the arches between, (thus retaining the form suggested by the construction,) a ceiling may be obtained, which would, I think, show handsomely, and probably favor the voice in speaking; especially if the joists run at right angles to the line of speech.

Section of Ceiling finished.

It will be perceived, that each of these two modes of fire-proofing has its own peculiar advantages and facilities of adaptation.   The choice between them should be determined, partly by the style of Architecture, partly by the destination of the edifice.   While groined vaults are clearly unsuited to the Post and Lintel manner,

* The arched ceilings in the school-rooms of the Girard College, (of which the size is fifty feet square and the height twenty-five feet,) are smoothly finished; and, in his final Report, the architect says:

"The reverberation of sound in these rooms, in consequence of their magnitude and their arch-formed ceilings, renders them wholly unfit for use; and unless a level ceiling is thrown in at the top of the cornice, or some other means employed to destroy the reverberation, they can never be used for the purposes of school or recitation-rooms.   They are, however, constructed in exact accordance with the will, and these results were anticipated in the earliest stages of the work; but as Mr. Girard left no discretionary power in reference to this part of the design, we were compelled to take the letter of the will as our guide, let the results be what they might."—*Final Report, Note to* p. 27.

The chemical lecture-room in the east wing of the Smithsonian building is very nearly the same size as one of these recitation-rooms, and its ceiling, thirty-two feet high, is a Norman groined vault, intersected by ribs with deep mouldings.   It is now completed and ready for use; and is found to be perfectly adapted for public speaking, and free from any unpleasant reverberation.

the iron beam is sometimes appropriate enough in Arch Architecture, especially in the Norman style.

The materials necessary to establish a definitive judgment as to the relative cost of different styles of Architecture, are daily accumulating in our country. Meanwhile, as the general result of inquiries and investigations, which, as chairman of a committee having in charge an important erection, it became my duty to make, I state my opinion, that, in the great majority of instances where a public edifice is required, stamped with a distinctive architectural manner and embellished with more or less of characteristic ornament, some phase of the two chief varieties of Arch Architecture, the Norman or Gothic, will be found not only the most appropriate style of construction, but the most economical also.

In simple private dwellings, or in public buildings without any pretension to architectural style or enriching ornament, the plain, every-day, square-headed, brick-and-mortar manner of modern times, is, without doubt, the least costly and embarrassing.

To what extent, in public Architecture, embellishment may with propriety be carried, is a question to which the answer must be of a general character only. Prescott, speaking of the degree of civilization which may justly be ascribed to the ancient Aztecs, says:

"Architecture is a sensual gratification, and addresses itself to the eye; it is the form in which the resources of a semi-civilized people are most likely to be lavished."*

From this remark, or at least from the spirit in which it will be interpreted, I dissent; just as I should dissent from the argument of any one, who, in discussing the influence exerted by one of the most civilizing of the arts, should say: "Music is a sensual gratification and addresses itself to the ear." The effect of chaste beauty in art is always humanizing. We are civilized through our senses. And life would be saddened and chilled, if of the thousand bright and gladdening influences that cheer its paths, all those were to be shut out as unworthy that impart gratification to the senses alone, and are not addressed directly to the intellect.

But if Prescott designs to speak of bootless expenditure and meretricious ornament only, then we may cordially concur in the sentiment, that these mark a half barbarous age. The simply elegant and the becoming in dress should not be despised, in man or woman. But it would undoubtedly be a retrograde movement in civilization, if there were to come into fashion among us the gorgeous apparel worn by the great and the wealthy three hundred years ago; by the nobles, for example, of the courts of Henry and of Francis, when they followed their respective monarchs to the celebrated "Field of the Cloth of Gold;" of whom quaintly says the old chronicler:† "Many, I doubt not, carried thither on their shoulders their castles, forests and lands."

* *Conquest of Mexico*, vol. i, p. 155.   † Du Bellay.

And thus, too, it would assuredly be an indication of a return to semi-civilization, were the taste of our modern day so far to depart from simplicity and utilitarian economy as to call up and reproduce among us the rich extravagance of the Florid Gothic ; the cathedral of Beauvais or Mechlin, for instance, or the town-hall of Louvain, or any other of those marvellous creations of an exuberant fancy, running riot in its inordinate love of decoration.   Whether in the category is to be included a style the reverse of this in its entire character and effects, yet equalling or surpassing it in the cost of its purest examples; whether we are to set it down as an indication of barbaric taste, to appropriate one or two millions for a marble copy of that temple model, of which the ruins, on the Athenian Acropolis or elsewhere on classic ground, still dazzle modern eyes, is a question which some will consider of more difficult solution.   To judge from the past, it would be no superfluous precaution in any man who is bequeathing even a princely fortune for a benevolent purpose, to introduce into his will a clause restricting the amount which his executors shall expend in building.

Should Congress hereafter decide upon the erection of additional public buildings, I commend to their consideration the results above set forth; and I advise, that in any Bill providing for such erection, a provision be inserted, limiting to a specific amount per cubic foot of available contents, the cost of the projected building.

Circular Window, North Front, Smithsonian Institution.

CHAPTER IX.

THE SMITHSONIAN INSTITUTION BUILDING: EXEMPLIFYING THE STYLE OF THE TWELFTH CENTURY.

THE building erected in the City of Washington for the Smithsonian Institution, stands on a lot of ground containing about nineteen acres, a grant from the General Government; being a portion of what is usually called the Mall, a tract of public land lying directly west of the Capitol, and extending from the Capitol grounds to the Potomac. The immediate site of the building is elevated about twenty feet above the average level of Pennsylvania Avenue, and commands a good view of the city and its principal public buildings.

The style of Architecture selected is that of the last half of the twelfth century; the latest variety of the rounded style, as it is found immediately anterior to the merging of that manner in the early Gothic.* In his general design and in most of his details, the architect has adhered, with a good deal of strictness, to the forms and characteristic enrichments of the period to which this style is referable. The general feeling, however, which pervades his design, especially in the principal towers, is that of a somewhat later era, when all lingering reminiscences of the Post and Lintel manner had been shaken off, and the ruling principles of Arch Architecture were recognized and carried out. I am not acquainted with any actual example, yet remaining from what has been variously called the Lombard, the Norman, the Romanesque and the Byzantine school, with which the Smithsonian building will not favorably compare. In so far as the architect has permitted himself to innovate upon ancient precedents from the style in which he designed, he has done so, in my judgment, with discretion and advantage.

* The Committee appointed by the Board of Regents to select plans for the Smithsonian building, reported, that, out of thirteen designs submitted to them, they had "unanimously selected two, by Mr. James Renwick, junior, of New York City; one of these designs being in the Decorated Gothic style, the other in the Norman;" and they go on to say, that they "recommend to the Board for their adoption, as the simpler and less ornate of the two, the latter, being the Norman plan. The plan thus recommended by the Committee, with certain modifications tending to lessen its cost, was adopted by the Board.

The Gothic plan above referred to being the second choice of the Committee, is given (plate facing page 99) as a good specimen of Middle-age or Decorated Gothic. Though more showy than the plan adopted, yet, chiefly in consequence of its compact form, it was not more costly.

SMITHSONIAN INSTITUTION, FROM THE NORTH EAST.

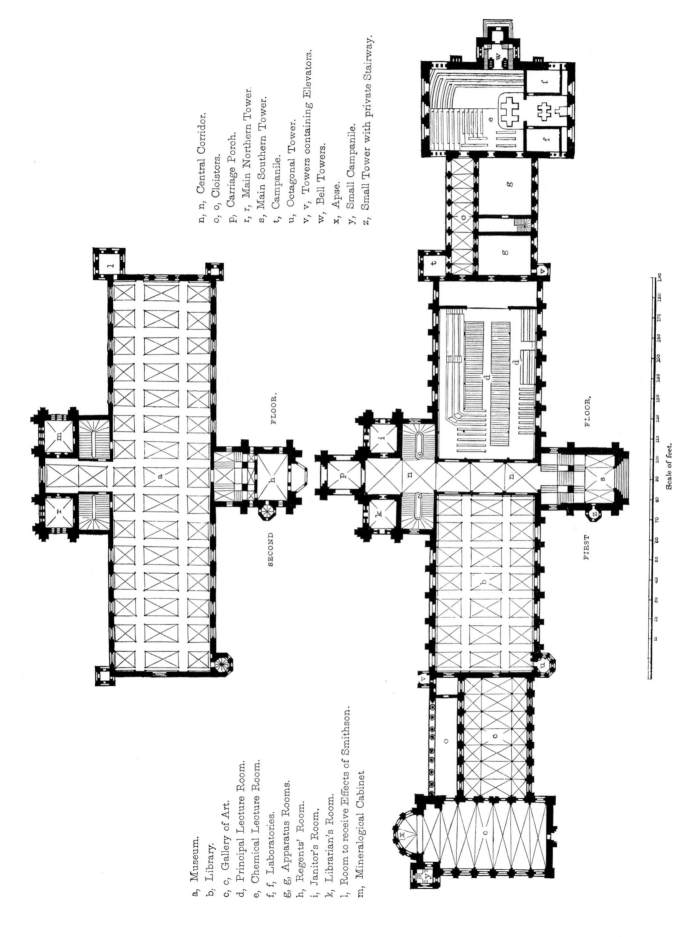

a, Museum.
b, Library.
c, c, Gallery of Art.
d, Principal Lecture Room.
e, Chemical Lecture Room.
f, f, Laboratories.
g, g, Apparatus Rooms.
h, Regents' Room.
i, Janitor's Room.
k, Librarian's Room.
l, Room to receive Effects of Smithson.
m, Mineralogical Cabinet.

n, n, Central Corridor.
o, o, Cloisters.
p, Carriage Porch.
r, r, Main Northern Tower.
s, Main Southern Tower.
t, Campanile.
u, Octagonal Tower.
v, v, Towers containing Elevators.
w, Bell Towers.
x, Apse.
y, Small Campanile.
z, Small Tower with private Stairway.

SECOND FLOOR.

FIRST FLOOR.

Scale of feet.

GROUND-PLANS, SMITHSONIAN INSTITUTION.

The semichcular arch, stilted,* is employed throughout, in doors, windows and other openings. The windows are without elaborately traceried heads. The buttresses are not a prominent feature, and have no surmounting pinnacles. The weather-mouldings consist of corbel-courses, with bold projection. The towers are of various shapes and sizes; and the main entrance from the north, sheltered by a carriage porch, is between two, of unequal height.

The design, as may be seen by an inspection of the ground-plans, consists of a main centre building two stories high, and two wings, of a single story, connected by intervening ranges; each of these latter having, on the north, or principal front, a cloister, with open stone screen.

The main building has, in the centre of its north front, two towers, of which the higher reaches an elevation of 145 feet.† On its south front it has a single massive tower, 37 feet square, including buttresses, and 91 feet high.‡ On its northeast corner stands a double Campanile, 17 feet square, and, measured to the top of its finial, 117 feet high;§ at its southwest corner, an Octagonal Tower,‖ finished with open work in its upper portion; and at its southwest and northwest corners are two smaller towers, fitted up with elevators, by which heavy weights can be conveyed to any part of the main building without being carried up the stairways. There are nine towers in all, including a small one at each wing.

The extreme length of the building, from east to west, including the porch of the east wing, is 447 feet. Its greatest breadth, across the centre of the main building and towers, and including the carriage porch, is 160 feet. The east wing is 82 feet by 52, and 42½ feet high to the top of its battlement; the west wing, including its projecting apse, is 84 feet by 40, and 38 feet high; and each of the connecting ranges, including its cloister, is 60 feet by 49. The main building is 205 feet by 57, and, to the top of its corbel-course, 58 feet high.

The east wing contains a small lecture-room, with raised seats and a gallery; also a Laboratory opening into the lecture-room by sliding doors, and having a mezzanine story above, for apparatus. Beneath is a basement, for forges, furnaces, &c. The lecture-room will seat from three to four hundred persons; and is designed for lectures

---

* When the point from which a semicircular arch is struck, is above its points of impost, the arch is said to be *stilted*, and, in that case, the mouldings between these two levels (its centre, namely, and its point of impost on either side) are continued vertically, except, indeed, in the horse-shoe variety, in which they incline inwardly. The effect of the Norman Arch, stilted, may be seen in the cuts representing the windows of the Smithsonian building. (See pages 75 and 80.) A semicircular arch not stilted has, as a general rule, a flat and clumsy air.

† See Frontispiece.

‡ It is represented on plate facing page 43.

§ This Campanile and one of the small towers containing elevators are shown on plate facing page 19.

‖ The plate showing this tower faces page 107.

on chemistry, natural philosophy, or such other branches of science as require, for their illustration, experiments that cannot properly be seen at a considerable distance. The distance, in this room, from the remotest seat to the lecturer's table is 44 feet.

Gallery of Art.

The east connecting range, with a half story above, has another Laboratory, and various rooms for apparatus.

The west wing* and west connecting range are to be occupied, throughout, as a Gallery of Art.

The upper room in the main building, unbroken by corridor or stairway, 200 feet by 52 in the clear, is destined for a museum, and is to receive the collection of the Exploring Expedition, and other collections which have been transferred by the Government to the Institution. The ground-floor, crossed centrally by a corridor, has, on one side, the library, and, on the other, the principal lecture-room, each 90 feet by 52, in the clear. The library, with its gallery, is capable of receiving a hundred thousand volumes; and the lecture-room, of seating from eight hundred to a thousand persons.

The central northern towers contain rooms for a Janitor; a Librarian's room; a room to receive the effects of Smithson, a mineralogical cabinet, and two artists' studios. The principal staircase ascends between these towers and the main building. The central tower on the south has, below, the staircase for the southern entrance; on the first story the Board of Regents' room, and, above that, the Secretary's room and a geological cabinet.† A small

* It is shown on plate facing page 75.

† An inspection of the law organizing the Smithsonian Institution will show the extent of accommodation by that Act required to be provided; and will enable the public to judge how far its requirements have been complied with. The Act provides, that the Institution building shall contain:

1. "Rooms or halls, for the reception and arrangement, upon a liberal scale, of objects of Natural History, including a geological and mineralogical cabinet.

2. "A chemical laboratory.

3. "A library.

4. "A gallery of Art.

5. "The necessary lecture-rooms;" and

6. An apartment in which "the minerals, books, manuscripts and other property of James Smithson shall be preserved separate and apart from the other property of the Institution."

OCTAGONAL TOWER, SMITHSONIAN INSTITUTION

turret, running up the centre of its western face, affords a private stairway to these rooms. The Campanile and Octagonal towers also contain staircases.

The material employed is a lilac grey variety of freestone, found in the New Red Sandstone formation, where that formation crosses the Potomac, near the mouth of Seneca Creek, one of its tributaries, and about twenty-three miles above Washington. In quality it is probably not surpassed by any freestone ever used in the United States; and its tint harmonizes well with the gravity of style and purpose appertaining to the Institution building.*

The building is erected in the most substantial manner. The foundation walls under the main central towers are twelve feet thick at bottom, gradually diminishing to five feet six inches at the surface of the ground, and are sunk eight feet deep. The foundations of the rear central tower, excavated to the same depth, are ten feet, diminishing to five feet; of the Campanile and Octagonal towers, also ten feet, diminishing to five; and six feet deep. The thickness of the walls of the main building, above the water-table, is two feet and a half in the first story, and two feet in the second, exclusive of buttresses, corbel-courses and other similar external projections, and exclusive, also, of an internal lining wall of brick, of the thickness of a single brick, tied, at intervals, to the wall, and designed to plaster to. The walls of the wings are two feet thick; of the central towers, three feet and a half thick in the first story, diminishing to two feet in the highest story. Inverted arches of hard brick are turned under all the openings of the foundation. Groined arches are turned under the central towers, the Campanile and Octagonal towers, and the tower of the west wing.

All the copings, cornices, battlements, window-jambs, mullions, sills, and, in general, all the stone-work of similar character, is tied together with iron clamps, leaded.

The basements to contain the heating-furnaces, also the Janitor's rooms and the room to receive Smithson's personal effects, are fire-proofed. The rest of the building is only partially so. A pine floor covered, two inches thick, with cement, is carried under the roofs of the whole building; and the floors, where they are not fire-proofed, have a deafening of lime, clay, and sand. The central staircases, in front and in rear, are of stone, to the museum floor. The floor of the Gallery of Art, embracing the west wing and its connecting range; of the laboratory, including the east wing and part of its connecting range; of the central hall and the vestibule; also the floors of the basement under the laboratory, under the central towers, under the Campanile and other towers; also the cloisters; are all flagged with North River flagging. The floor of the principal lecture-room is also laid with flags, supported on brick cross-walls.

---

* For further particulars regarding this building-stone, see Appendix. By reference to the details there given it will be perceived, that this material, infinitely superior as it is to that heretofore used for public buildings in Washington, has been obtained at less than half the cost of the latter.

The ceilings of the Museum, Library, Gallery of Art, and the rooms connected with them; also of the main central hall, the entrance porch, the rooms in the central front towers, the rooms in the Octagonal and Campanile towers; also the ceilings of the principal staircase, halls and vestibules, and of the Regents' room; are all groined and ribbed with deep Norman mouldings. The ceiling of the principal lecture-room is flat, and heavily panelled with deep ribs. It is confidently expected that, by this mode of finishing these ceilings, strictly according as it does with the Norman manner, all unpleasant reverberation will be avoided.*

The roofs, except of the connecting ranges, are slated. In the case of the east wing this was important; as all roofs whence rain-water, for chemical purposes, is to be derived, should be of slate. The ranges are roofed with leaded tin, laid in furrows.

The face of the building is finished in ashlar, laid in courses from ten to fifteen inches in height, and having an average bed of nine inches.

Of this spacious edifice the east wing and the adjacent connecting range are now† completed and occupied; while the west wing and its connecting range are completed externally, and will be ready for occupation next season. The foundations of the main building, including its towers, are laid; and it is designed to place the whole of this part of the structure under roof before next winter.

By the terms of the contract, the entire building is to be completed, fitted up and furnished on or before the 19th of March, 1852; and the Building Committee see no reason to doubt, that these terms will be strictly complied with.

The grounds of the Institution are planted with trees and shrubs, comprising about a hundred and fifty species, chiefly American; and are enclosed with a hedge, protected by a temporary fence. The hedge consists of *Pyrocanthus*, *Osage Orange*, *Cherokee Rose*, and *Hawthorn*, respectively, on the four sides of the lot: investigations and inquiries on that subject having satisfied the Committee, that the climate of Washington is favorable to the growth and maintenance of hedges, and that, for a moderate expense, a permanent and beautiful enclosure may thus be secured.

Designs submitted by the architect for cast-iron gateways, necessary to connect the Institution grounds with the adjoining streets, have been adopted.‡

The two perspective views of the building§ convey a pretty accurate impression of its general character and appearance.

* It has already been stated, that the Chemical lecture-room, with a vaulted ceiling 32 feet high, finished as above, is found to be free from all undue or injurious reverberation.

† February, 1849.

‡ The tail-piece to this chapter, on the next page, shows the principal gateway, on the centre of the southern line of the grounds, with the towers of the Institution building in the distance.

§ One, showing the southern front, faces this page; the other, exhibiting the north or principal front, faces the commencement of this chapter.

SMITHSONIAN INSTITUTION, FROM THE SOUTH WEST

J. Renwick Jr Architect.

Lith by Sarony & Major 117 Fulton St. N.Y.

It will be the first edifice, in the style of the twelfth century and of a character not ecclesiastical, ever erected in this country.

Dating from that period, which, in a previous chapter, I have recommended as a profitable field of study and fitting point of departure, whence to reach an Architecture suited to our own country and our own time, the manner of the Smithsonian building supplies a valuable commentary on much that has here been said.   Difficult as it is fully to convey by words, or even by aid of the pencil, a distinct idea of the feeling and principles which lie at the base of each distinctive style, I esteem myself fortunate, in the present instance, in being able to refer to an actual example, at our Seat of Government, the architect of which seems to me to have struck into the right road, to have made a step in advance, and to have given us, in his design, not a little of what may be fitting and appropriate in any manner, (should the genius of our country hereafter work such out,) that shall deserve to be named as a National Style of Architecture for America.

Southern Gateway, Smithsonian Institution.

APPENDIX.

APPENDIX.

NOTE A.

THE facts relative to the selection of building-stone for the Smithsonian Institution, taken in connection with the character of material previously used in the City of Washington, are both remarkable and instructive.

There existed, on the very banks of the Chesapeake and Ohio Canal, and about twenty-three miles, by the tow-path, from Washington, a freestone from the same geological formation which furnished, at Little Falls, building material for Trinity Church, New York, and equalling, if it do not exceed, that material, in durability, fineness of grain and beauty of color. Recent quarryings have shown, that this freestone, not excelled in quality by any, perhaps, in the United States, is found in inexhaustible quantity, and can be obtained with great facility. Contracts have been made to deliver it in Washington, at *twenty cents* per cubic foot of dimension stone.

Yet, up to the period when the Smithsonian building was commenced, this excellent material had not been employed in the construction of a single edifice, public or private, in the city. Private dwellings were chiefly constructed of brick; and the public buildings erected by the General Government, were built (with a single exception, the General Post Office) of a freestone so faulty, imperfect and perishable, that if it had been offered to the Committee charged with the construction of the Smithsonian Institution, delivered on the ground for nothing, they would, even then, have rejected it. This material is found near the Potomac, about sixty miles below Washington, and was, necessarily, brought up stream all that distance. It has cost the Government, delivered in the city, never less than *forty-five* cents, often *fifty*, per cubic foot of dimension stone.

The result to the Government has been much more than the mere pecuniary loss incurred by paying nearly twice and a half as much for building material, as they ought to have paid. There is hardly a single block of stone in any one of the edifices referred to, that is not, more or less, faulty or blemished. The innumerable clay-holes which pervade their surface, have been filled up with large quantities of putty; and it is evident to a common observer, that buildings which were calculated, by the character of their workmanship, to endure for ages, are already gradually decaying, for lack of judgment in the selection of their material.

It would be difficult to find a more striking proof of the importance, before commencing any expensive public erection, of causing to be instituted, by some competent person, a careful exploration of the surrounding country, not only where quarries have been opened, but wherever the geological formation holds out promise of the material desired.

Such an examination was set on foot by the Building Committee of the Smithsonian Institution; and resulted in great advantage, not only to the Institution for which they were acting, but to the City of Washington; nor, probably, to these alone; for, if Congress hereafter decide to erect additional public buildings at the Metropolis, the information obtained will essentially benefit the Government also. It is quite certain, that the material which now disfigures the architecture of the Treasury Building and the Patent Office, will never again be employed in any public edifice in Washington.

The course pursued by the Committee in reference to this subject, is set forth in their Report to the Board of Regents, dated December 7, 1847; to wit, in the following extract:

"The Board will perceive that the Committee, in discharge of their duty, were led into a somewhat extended field of inquiry, especially as regards building material; and that they have been enabled to collect, and have duly recorded, a large amount of detailed information on this subject essential to their own guidance, but also, they believe, important to the public generally, and especially to the Government, if Congress should decide to erect any other public buildings in this city. They caused to be examined the various marble, and granite, and freestone quarries within a moderate distance of Washington, having been fortunate enough to engage the services of a gentleman of practical experience as a geologist, and who tendered these services gratuitously, his necessary travelling and other expenses only being paid.

"The examination embraced the chief marble and granite quarries of Maryland; the freestone quarries of Acquia Creek, Virginia, whence the material has been drawn for the construction of the Capitol, President's house, Treasury Building, and other public structures in this city; and the freestone quarries of the upper Potomac, chiefly in the vicinity of Seneca Creek, on the banks of the Chesapeake and Ohio Canal, and about twenty-three miles from the city.

"The results of this examination, as contained in reports made by the geologist, and which will be found spread at large on our journal, were briefly these:

"1st. That the marble quarries of Maryland, chiefly in the vicinity of the village of Clarksville, about thirteen miles from Baltimore, on the line of the Susquehanna Railroad, contain two qualities of marble: one fine-grained and of beautiful uniform color, approaching the character of statuary marble; the other, of inferior quality, similar to the Sing Sing marble employed in New York, in Grace Church and other public structures, of a somewhat coarse and highly crystalline structure, and known to the quarrymen here under the name of 'alum limestone.' The former was confidently recommended as a building material equal in durability to any in the world; the latter was pronounced inferior, both in beauty and durability, yet capable of furnishing a very lasting material, if the selection was made with care. Being less tough than the finer-grained variety, it was thought less suitable for ornaments having bold projections, and somewhat liable to chip off where there was much undercutting.

"2d. That the granite quarries of Maryland, in the vicinity of Woodstock, on the line of the Baltimore and Ohio Railroad, and about sixteen miles beyond the Relay House, furnish a granite equal to that of Quincy, and not excelled, for beauty of appearance, compactness of structure and uniformity of color, texture, and composition, by any granite in the United States; splitting, also, with remarkable facility, so that on a block, twelve or fourteen feet in length, the face of cleavage may not vary more than a single inch from a true level; in short, a building material of unsurpassed durability and uniformity, and to which, as to the finer grained marble in the Clarkesville quarries, no possible objection, except on the score of expense, could be found; unless, indeed, it be considered one, that in this material the effect of light and shade from projecting surfaces is in a measure lost, while in marble and good tinted freestone every shadow is sharply marked.

" 3d. That the Acquia creek freestone, heretofore used in public buildings in Washington, is a material not to be trusted to, being pervaded by dark specks of the protoxide and peroxide of iron, which in peroxidating acquire a yellowish or reddish color, and having occasional clay holes, such as disfigure the Treasury and the Patent Office.   A portion of this freestone was, indeed, considered durable and free from material blemish; but the chance of actually procuring it free from disfiguring spots and stains, was considered so uncertain, that it was recommended to refrain from using it in the Institution building.

" 4th. That the freestone of the upper Potomac, in the vicinity of Seneca creek, and found in quarries close to the line of the Chesapeake and Ohio canal, is the best and most durable of all the Potomac freestones.

" The lilac-gray variety found in the Bull Run quarry, twenty-three miles from Washington, was especially recommended, and pronounced to be equal, if not superior, to that supplied for Trinity Church, New York, from the quarries of New Jersey.

" In regard to this latter material, it was stated that it possessed a quality that should especially recommend it to the attention of builders.   When first quarried it is comparatively soft, working freely before the chisel and hammer; but by exposure it gradually indurates, and ultimately acquires a toughness and consistency that not only enables it to resist atmospheric vicissitudes, but even the most severe mechanical wear and tear.   Thus, on the tow-path of the aqueduct, near Seneca creek, over which horses and mules have been travelling almost daily for upwards of twenty years, this freestone was found still unimpaired. Even the corners around which the heavy lock-gates swing, showed no signs of chipping or decay: and on the perpendicular wall of the aqueduct, where the water is continually oozing through the joints and trickling down its face, forming an incrustation of carbonate of lime, this freestone was observed, where the calcareous crust had scaled off, with the grooves and ridges of the surface still nearly as distinct as when the blocks first came from the hands of the stone-mason, more than twenty years ago.

" The rare and valuable quality possessed by this freestone, of hardening by exposure to the weather, and which may be due to iron in its composition, passing from a lower to a higher degree of oxidation, is occasionally found in building-stone on the continent of Europe; as, for example, in a calcareous freestone which has been excavated for centuries from St. Peter's mountain, near Maestrich, in Belgium.   It is highly prized wherever found, as this peculiarity permits the freestone to be wrought at considerably less expense than either granite or marble, and imparts to it a durability increasing with age.

" Further to test the durability of these various building materials under exposure to the vicissitudes of the seasons, specimens of each, and also of other building-stones from New York and elsewhere, were handed to a gentleman of this city experienced in chemistry, and having a laboratory at command, and he was requested to subject these to a process recommended by Brard, a French chemist, and described in the ' Annales de Chimie et Physique;' according to which, the crystallization of the sulphate of soda is substituted for the freezing of water; and thus, by artificial means, the action of the elements on these materials—the alternate freezing and thawing to which the external component of a building is in this climate annually subjected—is in a measure imitated.*   The result—which, however, in consequence of the short time which could be allowed for the process, must be considered an approximation only to the

---

* See Note B of this Appendix.

truth—is given in a report from the gentleman in question. The specimens were reduced to inch cubes; and it was found, after four weeks, that a cube of granite had lost about *one-third of a grain ;* a cube of the fine-grained marble about *one-fifth of a grain;* a cube of the best quality of the 'alum-stone,' or coarser-grained marble, *half a grain to a grain and a half;* and a cube of freestone from the Patent Office, which, however, was judged not to be a fair average specimen of the Acquia creek freestones, lost *eighteen grains and a half.* Freestone from Trinity Church lost from *two-thirds of a grain* to about *a grain and a half.* The brown Connecticut stone, freely used in New York, lost from *fourteen* to nearly *twenty-five* grains. Coarse-grained New York marble, from Mount Pleasant, lost *nearly a grain ;* Nova Scotia coarse-grained sandstone about *two grains ;* while Pennsylvania blue limestone lost little over *a quarter of a grain.*

"As to the relative cost of Maryland granite, Maryland marble, fine-grained and coarse-grained, Acquia creek freestone and Seneca creek freestone, it was found, from the report of the geologist and from actual offers made to the Committee by owners of quarries, and which will be found recorded in the journal of the Committee, to be, per cubic foot of dimension stone delivered in Washington, as follows :

"1st. For coarse-grained marble with large crystals, commonly called 'alum-stone,' from *fifty* to *sixty cents,* according to quality.

"2d. For fine-grained marble, the lowest offer was *seventy* cents.

"3d. For granite, *forty-six* cents.

"4th. For Acquia creek freestone, *forty* cents. The material used in the public buildings in Washington, in blocks of ordinary size, has cost from *forty-five* to *fifty* cents.

"5th. For Seneca freestone, the lilac-gray variety, from Bull Run quarry, *twenty* cents. A contract has been made by a gentleman of Washington, not connected with the Institution, to have stone from the Seneca creek quarries delivered to him in the city at that price.

"East Chester marble was offered at *seventy-five* cents.

"Such is a brief summary of the measures adopted by the Committee, and of the information collected by them, and which will be found in detail on their journal, on the important subject of building material."

Of the bids received for the erection of the Smithsonian building, fourteen in number, the lowest were,

To erect the building of marble, *ashlar* finish, ...	$228,500
And of Seneca freestone, *ashlar* finish, ...	205,250
Difference, in favor of freestone.	$23,250

The marble intended in the above bid was the coarse-grained variety with large crystals, above-mentioned as usually termed "alum-stone." With a belief on the minds of the Committee that the Seneca freestone was as durable as this variety of marble, and a doubt whether its tint did not even better assort with the Norman style of Architecture adopted than did that of the marble ; they deemed it inexpedient to expend twenty-three thousand dollars additional, to procure this latter material. They accordingly accepted the second bid ; and the lilac-gray variety of freestone found in the quarries of Bull Run, has been employed for the Smithsonian building.

Note B.

BRARD'S PROPOSAL TO IMITATE THE ACTION OF FROST ON BUILDING MATERIALS—LIABILITY OF THE PROCESS TO INACCURACY—DR. PAGE'S REPORT ON THE SUBJECT—TABLE OF RESULTS OF EXPERIMENTS.

It occurred to a French chemist, M. Brard, that the action of alternate freezing and thawing upon building materials, and which is the chief cause of their decay and disintegration, might be artificially imitated; so as to produce upon them, in a comparatively short time, the crumbling effect exerted by the vicissitudes of the seasons, under natural circumstances, throughout a long term of successive winters: and that, in this way, the comparative durability of building materials, or, in other words, their power to resist, unimpaired, the action of the elements, might be determined, at least with approximating accuracy. He proposed to immerse the building material to be tested, in a solution of sulphate of soda, saturated in the cold, so as to allow the crystals of the salt to be formed in its pores and over its surface. According to the natural process, the water absorbed by any building material, in freezing or crystallizing, exerts, by its expansive power, a disintegrating effect upon the particles of the stone. Brard sought to exert upon it a similar influence, by allowing the sulphate of soda to crystallize within its pores.

It has been proved by experiment, that, though crystals of sulphate of soda, unlike ice, sink in their own solution, and may therefore be supposed not to expand to the same extent as water in the act of freezing, yet, at the moment of congelation, there is, in the solution in question, considerable expansion. So far, then, the action of frost is imitated by Brard's process. It remains a question, however, how far the action of the salt upon various rocks may be of a chemical as well as a mechanical character; and to what extent this circumstance may disturb the accuracy of the result sought for.*

A mode of experiment less liable to error, though doubtless much more tedious, would be, to subject various building materials, carefully cut into cubes of equal size, to the natural action of frost, throughout one or more winters; thawing them as often as they were completely frozen; and collecting, with the greatest care, the sediment that should scale off each. In an ordinary winter, and in the latitude of New York, this alternate action of freezing and thawing could probably be repeated from fifty to a hundred times. The crumbling effect from the efflorescing process is, indeed, much more powerful than by the natural one: but even by the latter, it would probably be, in a single winter, sufficiently great, to supply useful materials for comparison.

It would be interesting, also, to compare the results obtained, under similar circumstances and from the same specimens, by the two different processes.

The time allowed to the Building Committee of the Smithsonian Institution before closing the contract, was not sufficient to permit the instituting of any protracted experiments. They decided, however, to test

---

* If a freestone of ordinary quality be boiled, for eight or ten hours, in a solution of sulphate of soda, adding water to supply the loss by evaporation, and the solution, at the end of that time, be tested with hydro-sulphuret of ammonia, it will show a precipitate, small but very perceptible; though the saline solution, similarly treated before boiling, gave no precipitate whatever.

various materials in their possession by Brard's process; and the results, alluded to in the preceding note, are given in detail, in the following

REPORT

TO THE BUILDING COMMITTEE OF THE SMITHSONIAN INSTITUTION ON THE ACTION OF FROST UPON CERTAIN
MATERIALS FOR BUILDING.

" Of the twenty-five specimens of stone submitted to me for examination with reference to their relative properties in resisting the disintegrating action of frost, I have been able to investigate but twenty-two; the remaining specimens, marked, respectively, 1, 9, 5 D, being too small to submit to the test. It was thought desirable to ascertain their specific gravities, with a view to determine if any connection existed between their densities and liability to dilapidation. The result leads us to infer that such relation does not exist, and that the texture of the stone, without reference to density, determines its frangibility under the influence of frost. Resort was had in these experiments to an *imitation* of the operation of freezing water after the process described by Brard, a French chemist, in the '*Annales de Chimie et Physique*,' vol. 38. The details of the process will presently be given.

"The absorption and subsequent freezing of water within the stone would have been a more energetic mode of action; but the undertaking would prove one of considerable practical difficulty, and, on the whole, not so reliable as an experiment, unless, perhaps, the circumstances were such as to admit of their exposure to *natural* freezing under favorable circumstances.

" The process of Brard consists in substituting the crystallization of the sulphate of soda for the freezing of water, and has met with the approval of many French architects and engineers, as the results accord with their experience. In the freezing or crystallization of water, the expansion is such, that the crystals float; while in the crystallization of sulphate of soda, and other soluble salts, the crystals sink in the solution; but, notwithstanding, the exertion of the crystalline forces of these salts is sufficient to produce decided impressions upon the hardest of building materials in a few weeks.

"The specimens of stone furnished me by your board were all numbered as according to the subjoined table; and it may be proper to remark, that their localities and respective values, as usually estimated, were unknown to me until after the results of the experiments had been laid before you and approved.

" Six numbered specimens were also handed to me, and are marked, respectively, 1 D, 2 D, &c. The specimens were cut into inch cubes; three of the whole number, being of insufficient size, were laid aside, as above mentioned. The cubical blocks, suspended by strings, to which the respective numbers upon labels were attached, were first immersed in a boiling solution of sulphate of soda, saturated when cold; and after remaining half an hour in the boiling liquid, they were removed and hung upon a frame over half-pint bowls, containing also a quantity of the cold saturated solution.

" In the course of twenty-four hours a considerable efflorescence was found upon the surface of each specimen, consisting of the crystals of the salt mixed with comminuted portions of the stone. These were washed off daily, by simultaneously immersing the stones in the solution in the bowls, and suffering them to remain there for a few minutes. This proceeding was repeated daily for one week, when it became necessary to deviate from Brard's directions, and to keep them in a moderate temperature, instead of a cold cellar, as he advises. It was obvious that the investigation would be exceedingly protracted unless the crystallization of the salt were promoted by moderate warmth, as by this time the detritus from some specimens was hardly visible.

" After the change, the process went on with greater rapidity; and at the end of four weeks the dipping was stopped, and the sediment or deposite in each bowl was carefully weighed, and furnished the results as given in the table. In some cases the comminution of the stone was exceedingly fine; and in the washing and decanting process, ample time was allowed for the deposite to settle after each washing, and the utmost care used in the subsequent operations of decanting, drying, and weighing. The time of one week for the operation of dipping the stones in the solution was not deemed sufficient, as the deposite from the marbles and some other varieties was hardly apparent; and it was therefore continued, as above stated, four weeks, and thus the slight errors of manipulation, if any occurred, are proportionally diminished.

DISINTEGRATING EFFECTS OF FROST UPON STONES USED FOR BUILDING MATERIALS.

SPECIMENS MARKED.		SPECIFIC GRAVITY.	LOSS BY FROST, IN GRAINS.
No. 1	Not tested; the specimen being too small, ...		
No. 2	Symington's close-grained marble, (similar to Worthington's,) . .	2.834	0.19
No. 3	Connecticut sandstone, coarsest-grained quality, ...	not ascertained.	14.36
No. 4	Dark red Seneca sandstone, (similar quality to Smithsonian stone,) .	2.672	0.70
No. 5	Symington's large crystal marble, ...	2.857	0.50
No. 6	Symington's blue limestone, ...	2.613	0.34
No. 7	Coarse, large crystal marble, Mt. Pleasant, New York, ...	2.860	0.91
No. 8	Port Deposite granite, ...	2.609	5.05
No. 9	Too small to examine.		
No. 10	Trinity sandstone, fine-grained and light colored, ...	not ascertained.	1.58
No. 11	Connecticut sandstone, finer-grained quality, ...	2.583	24.93
No. 12	Nova Scotia sandstone, coarse-grained, ...	2.518	2.16
No. 13	Light Seneca sandstone, dove-colored, ...	2.486	1.78
No. 14	Pennsylvania marble, close-grained, ...	2.727	0.35
No. 15	Pennsylvania blue limestone, ...	2.699	0.28
4 T C	Trinity Church light-colored, close-grained sandstone, New Jersey, . .	2.482	0.62
P O	Patent Office light sandstone, ...	2.230	18.60
S B	Soft brick, ...	2.211	16.46
H B	Hard brick, ...	2.294	1.07
1 D	Granite from Potomac Great falls, ...	Not ascertained.	0.35
2 D	Dark coarse sandstone, of Seneca aqueduct, Peter's quarry, . . .		5.60
3 D	Sandstone 4 miles above No. 2 D, Peter's, west of Beaver dam quarry, .		1.58
4 D	Dark sandstone, from quarry near Wood's residence, ...		3.94
5 D	Not tested, specimen being too small.		
6 D	Lower stratum, Beaver dam quarry, ...		1.72

" Respectfully submitted by

CHARLES G. PAGE."

WASHINGTON, D. C., *March* 5, 1847.

The Board of Regents of the Smithsonian Institution have had it in contemplation to cause to be instituted a series of more extensive experiments, to determine both the strength and the durability of the principal building materials throughout the United States. The results may hereafter be given to the public.